C000093018

understanding
our LGBTQ+
loved ones

RICHARD COHEN, M.A.

PATH PRESS

© 2022 Richard Cohen, M.A.
PATH Press

All rights reserved. Reproduction or translation of any part of this work beyond that permitted by Section 107 or 108 of the 1976 United States Copyright Act without the permission of the copyright owner is unlawful. Requests for permission or further information should be addressed to the Permissions Department, PATH Press.

This publication is designed to provide accurate and authoritative information in regard to the subject matter covered. It is sold with the understanding that the publisher is not engaged in rendering legal, accounting, or other professional service. If legal advice or other expert assistance is required, the services of a competent professional person should be sought. *From a Declaration of Principles jointly adopted by a committee of the American Bar Association and a committee of publishers.*

Without limiting the rights under copyright reserved above, no part of this publication may be reproduced, stored in or introduced into a retrieval system, or transmitted, in any form or by any means (electronic, mechanical, photocopying, recording or otherwise) without the prior written permission of the publisher of this book.

All rights reserved.
ISBN 978-1-7338469-8-1

Library of Congress Control Number: 2022917496

Cohen, Richard Alfred
October 1952

Layout design: Lisa DeSpain

PATH Press
P.O. Box 2315
Bowie, MD 20718
Tel. 301-805-5155
www.pathinfo.org

Printed in the United States of America

Contents

Dedication

I dedicate this book to all who pursue the truth in love.

It is my fervent hope that the information contained on the following pages will help to set the record straight, heal the broken-hearted, and help us learn how to love our LGBTQ+ family members and friends.

Acknowledgments

Thanks to my beautiful and faithful wife Jae Sook. I love and appreciate you.

Thanks to our three incredible children: Jarish, Jessica, and Alfred. You are all magnificent. I love you with all my heart.

Thanks to Carlos and Minty for having the vision to support this work and bring more love and truth into the world.

A heartfelt thanks to Andreina del Villar, my Angel. Without your loving support, this book would not have been born. We are family, forever.

Thanks to my beautiful and loving sister, Lyd Bonner. I appreciate you and Lloyd. You were always there for me, especially during the most difficult years.

Thanks to my dearest friends Mary Hamm and Phillip Schanker for your invaluable assistance in editing this book. You are the best!

Introduction

Truth without love is blind. Love without truth is deadly.

Richard Cohen

I t is time to bring understanding to the confusing issue of homosexuality. It is time to set the record straight and answer key questions, separating fact from fiction. Are people born gay, with same-sex attraction (SSA)? Did God make them that way? Did they choose to have SSA? Does God really love those who experience homosexual feelings? How do we respond to SSA family members, friends, and co-workers?

Understanding Our LGBTQ+ Loved Ones will illuminate basic truths about homosexuality and present simple suggestions that you may incorporate into your everyday life. It will offer rational answers about this very emotionally charged and volatile issue. *Through understanding and compassion, we may resolve, in a loving way, the controversies and confusion surrounding homosexuality.*

Why should *you* read a book about homosexuality? Why should *you* care? For just a moment, let me tell you why:

If you are a parent, you might have a child who one day proclaims, "I'm gay." If you are a son or daughter, you might have a mom who comes out and announces, "I'm a lesbian." If you are a brother or sister, cousin or relative, you might have a family member who says, "I'm gay." It's even possible that you might marry someone who one day reveals, after many years of marriage, "I'm gay."

I am a man who can give you an insider's look into homosexuality. I lived a gay life and had a male partner for three years. Today I am a heterosexual man; I have been married to my wife for over 42 years and we have three incredible adult children. I have also served as a psychotherapist for 35 years, and in the process, I have helped hundreds of men and women who experience *unwanted* same-sex attraction (SSA) fulfill their heterosexual dreams. Through healing seminars, online courses, and resource materials, I have helped thousands worldwide find freedom from unwanted homosexual feelings. I have also helped thousands of parents reconcile with their SSA loved ones, and in many cases, they were able to assist their children in coming out of homosexuality, even though they initially had no desire for change. This was accomplished by demonstrating unconditional love to their children in all the right ways (read *Gay Children, Straight Parents* for more details).

Imagine what it would feel like if *you* were in school, sitting at the lunch room table, and no one wanted to sit next to *you*, no one wanted *you* at their table—"faggot," "queer," "sissy," "dyke"—just some of the horrific names you might be called. No one wants to be seen with you.

Imagine *you* are at temple, church, or synagogue, and the Imam, Pastor, or Rabbi is preaching, "Homosexuality is a sin. They are going to hell." All the while, unbeknownst to your family and friends, *you* experience same-sex attractions. What's more, you never, ever wanted those desires in the first place. What do you do?

Imagine *you* prayed month after month, year after year, "God, please take these homosexual desires away! I don't want them. I never asked for them. Please dear God, if you care about me at all, take them away. I beg you." But the desires continue no matter how many tears you've shed, and no matter how much you prayed, you still experience same-sex attraction. What do you do?

These are just some of the experiences same-sex-attracted men and women go through on a daily basis, along with the slings and arrows of outrageous discrimination and persecution for feelings they never chose to have. What would *you* do if it were *your* son or daughter, brother or sister, family member or friend who experienced SSA? Today, almost every person knows someone who experiences same-sex attraction.

Here are some issues that I will share with you:

- How the gay phenomenon has become so pervasive in our world today
- The basic causes behind homosexual feelings
- Clues as to why five celebrities in the USA experience SSA
- How to use the right words that promote healing
- How to really love our LGBTQ+ family members and friends

It is quite possible that you have been indoctrinated into believing that people are "born gay and cannot change." If you think that anyone who experiences SSA cannot change his or her sexual attractions, you have been misled. Changing from homosexual to heterosexual is possible.

We have failed to understand what same-sex attracted men and women are going through. In the past, many of us treated people with SSA unfairly. We may have taunted and teased them. We may have rejected and judged them: "You're going to hell for this." "You're a fag." "Somebody ought to beat the queer out of you!" Instead of listening, instead of trying to understand what they are experiencing, we have hurt people who are already hurting.

Meanwhile, gay activists have organized, planned, and strategized how to gain public acceptance. They understand the reality that everyone needs to belong; everyone needs to be loved. Capitalizing on those needs, in the course of recent decades they have created a movement of empowerment. "We're queer, we're here, get used to it" were the cries of ACT-UP in the 1980s. By now we have gotten used to it. But should we? Of course each person's human rights and freedom to choose deserves respect, and is there more to this issue than meets the eye? And what about those who do not want to live a gay life? Don't they deserve our love and respect too?

These days teenagers are "coming out," declaring themselves to be LGBTQ+ (Lesbian, Gay, Bisexual, Transgender, Queer/Questioning) earlier than ever before. Many are identifying as non-binary, a term used to denote being different than one's gender, or identifying with both genders. More married men and women are announcing "I am gay" to their spouses and children. The fight for homosexual marriage in the USA was achieved in June 2015, and in many other countries throughout the world. New homosexual legislation is changing the moral fabric of society. Major motion pictures, television shows, and made-for-TV movies sympathetically portray the lives of LGBTQ+ men and women while demonizing people of religious faith as ill-informed and intolerant.

Regarding homosexuality, many religions are divided over two challenging issues: (1) should they allow active "gay" clergy to pastor their churches, and (2) should they endorse homosexual relationships? *Basically, we are straight and late!* By that I mean most of us failed to demonstrate compassion and understanding to those who experience same-sex attraction, and we are coming to this realization after the issue has been forced upon us.

As a former homosexual, and as a psychotherapist, I know this issue from the inside out. For many years I struggled with unwanted SSA and then lived for a while as a gay man. However, I had a burning desire in my heart to marry a woman and have children. Although the world told me that I was born with SSA and could not change, I never believed that for a minute. In my heart I knew that my destiny was to marry a woman and create a loving family. Today, I am living my dream. My wife and I have three incredible children. Our oldest son is a medical doctor and researcher; our daughter is a High School

English teacher; and our youngest son is an executive recruiter. My dream is now a reality!

It is sometimes said, "Whoever frames the debate, wins the debate." In recent decades, the Gay Rights Movement has strategically moved the debate about homosexuality from the realm of psychology and religion, and brought it into the arena of human rights and social justice. Why did they do this? Because they were sick and tired of being treated like second-class citizens. Before the 1970s, they found little hope for acceptance and understanding in the religious community or mental health profession. Instead they suffered constant ridicule and judgment for their homosexual desires—desires they never asked for in the first place. They were trapped with their backs against the wall, hurting, angry, resentful, and alone. What could they do? Who would help them? In the pages that follow, I will try and bring clarity to these questions and many more:

- **Chapter One**: A brief history of the "Gay Rights Movement" and what motivates their every decision and action.
- **Chapter Two**: How homosexual feelings develop in men and women, the real meaning behind same-sex attraction.
- **Chapter Three**: Clues to why five USA celebrities experience SSA: Olympic gold medal diver Greg Louganis, rock star Melissa Etheridge, former NBA player John Amaechi, former talk show host and actress Rosie O'Donnell, and former U.S. Department of Education Safe School Czar Kevin Jennings.
- **Chapter Four**: Terminology coined by homosexual activists alongside suggested language that may bring greater healing to those who experience SSA.
- **Chapter Five**: Simple and effective ways to love those who experience SSA, and thus help end the homosexual dilemma facing our nation and world.

This book is a basic primer about homosexuality. Consider it a Homosexuality 101 course. There are many other wonderful books on this subject. Please see the Recommended Reading list at the back of the book. These additional resources will give you an even deeper understanding about the causes behind same-sex attraction and the possibility of change.

I will repeat several concepts frequently throughout the book. Marketing strategies that are used to promote ideas on a daily basis impose beliefs upon us. For over five decades, regarding the issue of homosexuality, there has been only one side of this issue portrayed in the media. I would like to introduce you to another side. I will repeat often, and in many similar ways, that *people are not essentially born with SSA*. I will say again and again that *they never simply chose to have homosexual feelings*, and that *changing from homosexual to heterosexual is possible*.

In between the chapters you will find uplifting stories of transformation, demonstrating how a man or woman has made the change from homosexual to heterosexual desires. Through these narratives, you will come to understand more deeply the causes of SSA and how healing occurs. You may want to read all the chapters in the order presented, or reflect on them independently; it's entirely up to you. By the end I hope that you will have discovered how to love your SSA friend or family member in healthy ways.

Note: I use the term "gay" throughout the book. I view it as a socio-political term denoting someone who has accepted their SSA and decides to live a homosexual life. Also, the terms "lesbian, gay, bisexual, transgender, and queer" (LGBTQ+), are used for socio-political purposes. I do not believe there is any such thing as a "homosexual" person (viewed as a noun). There are only people who experience SSA (viewed as an adjective, describing someone's feelings).

Chapter One

A Brief History of the Gay Rights Movement

"Years of learning to hate myself didn't just slip away because I came out, and I still struggled with my feelings of self-loathing, feelings I would later come to understand as internalized homophobia. Unlike other traditional minorities in American society (Jews, people of color), gay people aren't raised by people like themselves and aren't connected to a community of people like themselves when growing up. As a result, we internalize the typically homophobic attitudes of those around us, and devaluing and demeaning homosexuality becomes part of our own self-image. This voice in your own head—the voice that constantly tells you that you are worthless—is the real enemy. Like a lot of gay people, I found that other people sometimes accepted me long before I had completely accepted myself" (*Momma's Boy, Preacher's Son,* Beacon Press, 2006, p. 121).

Kevin Jennings, Former Assistant Deputy Secretary,
Office of Safe & Drug Free Schools,
U.S. Department of Education

In this chapter, I will briefly detail the history of the Gay Rights Movement, expose the activists' strategic plan to normalize homosexuality in the USA and throughout the world, and disclose what fuels their agenda.

Prejudice against anyone who experiences SSA is wrong and needs to be corrected. However, embracing homosexual behavior as a normative condition is equally devastating. Why? Because it betrays the innate heterosexual potential of every precious man and woman in this world.

Why, when, and how did the Gay Rights Movement come into existence? What is the motivation behind their movement? How did homosexual activists achieve so much in such a short period of time? We need to understand how these activists influence our daily lives through the scientific community, religious institutions, media and entertainment industries, educational system, and the political process. Many in the Lesbian, Gay, Bisexual, Transgender, and Queer (LGBTQ+) community have enormous disposable incomes, as most of them do not have children. Money equals power!

Included in this chapter are the following topics:

- Historical Discrimination Leads to Guilt and Shame
- Birth of the Gay Rights Movement
- *After the Ball*, a Landmark Book that is Sometimes Called the "Homosexual Manifesto"
- Capturing the Scientific Community
- Religious Institutions Revise Theology: Historical Relativism
- Media and Entertainment Industry Promote Homosexuality
- Educational System Endorses LGBTQ+ Identity and Relationships
- Political Pressure to Enact Homosexual Legislation

Behind all the demands of homosexual activists are hurt little boys and girls who are longing for your love and acceptance. They never chose to experience SSA, and yet they incurred deep wounds when family, friends, and community rejected them. What were they to do? Who would defend them? Feeling hurt and pain, they organized and mobilized. They did all of this to win our love.

Historical Discrimination Leads to Guilt and Shame

Men and women who experience Same-Sex Attraction are often...

- Rejected by Religions
- Rejected by Governments
- Rejected by Educational Systems
- Rejected by the Scientific Community
- Rejected by their Family Members and Friends

We know throughout history that many religions have been the greatest perpetrators of judgment and discrimination against men and women who experienced homosexual feelings. Churches, mosques temples, and synagogues should have been the safest places for them, places of refuge and love, offering hope for healing. Instead, religious institutions were often appalling perpetrators of judgment and persecution toward those who experienced SSA. They quoted Leviticus 18:22 and Leviticus 20:13—homosexual acts are "detestable" and an "abomination"—while completely overlooking the fact that heterosexual behaviors outside of marriage are condemned in the same passages. This permitted people of faith to act self-righteously toward those who experience homosexual feelings.

The government also failed to protect SSA men and women, who often lost their jobs, homes, and lives. What about equal justice under law? What about the right to life, liberty and the pursuit of happiness? Why were some men and women who experience SSA unfairly treated in their work place or even in the privacy of their own homes?

Within the educational system, there has long been discrimination against students and teachers who experience SSA. Most same-sex attracted youth have been bullied and even assaulted because of their homosexual feelings, while no school ordinances and very few administrators protected them.

The scientific community has, in fact, flip-flopped. Prior to the early 1970s, many therapists successfully treated men and women who experienced unwanted same-sex attraction, helping them achieve their heterosexual dreams. However, in 1973, first the American Psychiatric Association and then the American Psychological Association abdicated from applying scientific facts by surrendering to the political pressure from homosexual activists both within and outside of their organizations. The scientific community truly failed the SSA population from that time on, caving into the political pressure of the day (more details about that will follow).

Often families also failed to understand, love, and support their SSA children and relatives. If a family member "came out," disclosing their SSA, they were often ostracized and disowned, which left them with nowhere to go. The heart of the family is supposed to be a place of warmth, safety, and love. When a family of a SSA child abandons her or him, s/he becomes an orphan left out in the cold.

Failure to love those who experience SSA by religious institutions, government agencies, educational systems, the scientific community, and their families, fueled the birth of the Gay Rights Movement. Consciously and unconsciously they have been saying:

- "We're mad as hell, and we're not going to take it anymore."
- "You've hurt us, not helped us."
- "All you did was condemn and mock us for feelings we never chose."
- "You say we're an abomination. You say that I can't live here. You say that I can't work here. You say I can't worship here. Where do I belong?"

Birth of the Gay Rights Movement

- Stonewall Inn Riots in New York City
- Gay Pride Month
- Birth of Homosexual Organizations
- *After the Ball:* Homosexual Manifesto

What were they to do? Where were they to go? Who would protect and defend them? In the 1960s, on the coattails of the Civil Rights Movement in the USA, homosexual activism was born (although various homophile organizations began springing up in the 1950s, such as the Mattachine Society and Daughters of Bilitis). On June 28, 1969, at about 1:20 a.m., at a homosexual bar called Stonewall Inn located in Greenwich Village, New York City, a historic event occurred, later to be known as the "Stonewall Inn Riots."

The police regularly broke into homosexual bars, harassing and beating up the customers. Finally, after years of misuse and abuse, they had had it. In the early morning hours of June 28, 1969, the LGBTQ+ patrons essentially stood up and said, "We're here, we're queer, and we're not going to take it anymore." They fought back. The battle between the Stonewall Inn customers and police lasted for several days. This became the spark that lit the fire throughout the USA and created the Gay Rights Movement. In every major city throughout the world, June or July is celebrated as "Gay Pride Month" to commemorate the 1969 Stonewall Inn Riots.

From that time they began to organize. Groups like The National Gay and Lesbian Task Force took shape. Many others soon followed: Lambda Legal Defense Fund (litigious arm of the homosexual movement), Human Rights Campaign (political action committee to change laws), and many more. They emulated strategies from the Civil Rights Movement, realizing they had to change public opinion about homosexuality in order to gain acceptance.

After the Ball, the Homosexual Manifesto

As this new homosexual rights movement gained momentum, activists got organized. In 1989 a remarkable book was published entitled *After the Ball: How America will conquer its fear and hatred of gays in the '90s* (all quotes used by permission from the publisher). Two gay men, Marshall Kirk and Hunter Madsen, wrote the book. Mr. Kirk was a researcher in neuropsychiatry, a logician, poet, and a 1980 graduate from Harvard University. Mr. Madsen was an expert in public persuasion tactics and social marketing who designed commercial advertising on Madison Avenue, and a 1985 graduate from Harvard.

In this landmark book, commonly known as the "Homosexual Manifesto," they mapped out a blueprint detailing how to indoctrinate the world into the innate-immutable mythology of homosexuality—"people are born gay and cannot change." The authors clearly state in *After the Ball* that they knew there was *insufficient scientific evidence that people are born with SSA.* Nonetheless, they decided to use this paradigm shift to gain public acceptance. This was their way of saying, "all is fair in love and war."

The authors of *After the Ball* cleverly took the debate about homosexuality out of the realm of religion and psychology and brought it into the realm of human rights and social justice. "Whoever frames the debate wins the debate." They strategically took the emphasis off of *homosexual behavior*—anal sex, oral sex, mutual masturbation, fisting—and placed it solely on *homosexual identity:* "We are born gay; God made us this way; being gay is not just what we do, it is who we are."

The political venue, using their mantra of human rights and social justice, was virgin territory for the promotion of homosexuality and public acceptance. It was a stroke of genius to shift the debate about homosexuality away from religious beliefs and psychological evidence, and move it to the realms of human rights and social justice. There they could influence public opinion and gain acceptance.

After the Ball is a remarkable strategic plan to homosexualize the world. In just a short period of time, the authors accomplished almost all of their goals. Let's look at the gist of their strategies:

> "This is a campaign of unabashed propaganda, firmly grounded in long-established principles of psychology and advertising" (*After the Ball*, Marshall Kirk and Hunter Madsen, Plume Book, New York, 1989, p. xxviii).

The authors had to address a hostile public who feared and often hated persons who experienced homosexual feelings. It is interesting that in their book Kirk and Madsen used the word "homo-hatred" instead of homophobia. I prefer the term homo-hatred myself; I believe it is more accurate. Homo-hatred describes a person who either speaks against or acts disparagingly toward a person with SSA. I do not hate or fear anybody who experiences homosexual feelings. On the contrary, I have the utmost love and respect for all persons who experience SSA. I simply believe, that according to the latest scientific evidence, *people are not essentially born with SSA and therefore change is possible*. I also believe that homosexual behavior is incompatible with natural law.

Homophobia is a misleading and inaccurate term; "phobia" represents an irrational fear of something or someone. Many of us do not fear or have prejudice toward people who identify as gay. However, LGBTQ+ persons easily label anyone with a principled disagreement about homosexual behavior as homophobic. This is incorrect based upon their own definition.

Kirk and Madsen discuss what most heterosexuals think about member of the LGBTQ+ community: "(1) hardly worth thinking about, (2) few in numbers, (3) easy to spot, (4) homosexual because of sin, insanity, or seduction, (5) kinky, loathsome sex addicts,

(6) unproductive and untrustworthy members of society, and (7) suicidally unhappy" (p.61).

> Kirk and Madsen decided to portray homosexuality as a *condition*, not as a *problem*, because *a problem can be fixed, but a condition must be accepted*. This, again, was part of their strategic plan: Homosexuals are not broken, therefore, they must be respected and accepted just as they are.

The authors realized that most people are extremely prejudiced against people who experience SSA and homosexual behavior. They analyzed the nature of prejudice—an illogical emotion, an automatic response to emotional conditioning, which is impervious to argument. Therefore prejudice is not a thought process, it is an emotion. In order for LGBTQ+ activists to be successful, they had to understand how prejudice works: (1) you can't argue it away, (2) it's not evil, (3) consciousness raising won't work, (4) prejudice is not an illness so it can't be cured by therapy, (5) it's not a conspiracy by sick or wicked people, (6) homosexual parades where homosexuals look extreme will not work, (7) learning to love and respect others will not work, (8) storming the barricades or picketing these people will not work, and (9) having sex in public places certainly will not work (pp. 113-114). So how would they move people from prejudice against homosexuality to acceptance of it?

Kirk and Madsen describe how prejudice works as an evolutionary function for survival and reproduction, in other words "survival of the fittest." We fear that which we don't understand, we make snap judgments without thinking, and thus the fight, flight or freeze response ensues. Homo-hatred is basically a learned pattern. Therefore what was learned can be unlearned. Connections made in the brain can be broken down and new connections made. "Prejudice is not a belief; it's a feeling. Argument can change beliefs, but not feelings. It's not useful in the treatment of homo-hatred" (p. 136).

"When you're very different, and people hate you for it, this is what you do: first you get your foot in the door, by being as similar as possible; then, and only then—when your one little difference is finally accepted—can you start dragging in your other peculiarities, one by one. You hammer in the wedge narrow end first. As the saying goes, Allow the camel's nose beneath the tent, and his whole body will soon follow" (p. 146).

Three-Stage Plan to Homosexualize the Nation:

(1) Desensitization
(2) Jamming
(3) Conversion

Kirk and Madsen declared that it is relatively easy to retrain the human brain to feel and react neutrally to a previously hated minority such as Lesbian, Gay, Bisexual, Transgender, and Queer persons. They developed a three-stage plan to accomplish this—Desensitization, Jamming, and Conversion.

First comes *desensitization*, which is the constant flooding of homosexual imagery into the culture through advertising, media, people sharing their stories, and homosexual related messages on a regular basis. This "flooding" of homosexual imagery will eventually desensitize us, until we think that homosexuality is just another "thing." "If straights can't shut the shower off, they may at least eventually get used to being wet" (p. 149). Today, everywhere you turn, there are images of LGBTQ+ persons on television, movies, Internet, newspapers, magazines, religion, science, schools, and politics.

Second is *jamming*, which can be thought of as throwing sand in a watch mechanism, and thereby preventing prejudice. "Jamming makes use of the rules of Associative Conditioning (the psychological process whereby, when two things are repeatedly juxtaposed, one's feelings about one thing are transferred to the other, e.g., picture-label

15

pair) and Direct Emotional Modeling (the inborn tendency of human beings to feel what they perceive others to be feeling)" (p. 150). An example of picture-label pair would be Oprah Winfrey embracing Ellen DeGeneres. A person might think, "I don't like Ellen because she's a lesbian. But Oprah likes Ellen, and I like Oprah, so I guess I'll like Ellen."

"Our effect is achieved without references to facts, logic, or proof…through repeated infralogical emotional conditioning, his bigotry can be alloyed in exactly the same way, whether he is conscious of the attack or not" (pp. 152-153).

Third and last is *conversion,* where the wheels of the watch turn in the opposite direction. "We mean conversion of the average American's emotions, mind, and will, through a planned psychological attack, in the form of propaganda fed to the nation via the media. We mean 'subverting' the mechanism of prejudice to our own ends—using the very processes that made America hate us to turn their hatred into warm regard—whether they like it or not. Put briefly, if Desensitization lets the watch run down, and Jamming throws sand in the works, Conversion reverses the spring so that the hands run backward" (pp. 153-154). This was their long-range goal, using the media to convert the public to full acceptance of homosexuality.

Most of us have been reprogrammed through this brilliant strategy. Here's how someone might unknowingly be reoriented through this reprogramming: "Well, I learned that homosexuality is normal and people are born gay. I was the bigot. I contributed to their suffering. Now, I love Ellen DeGeneres. I think she's just great. I love Greg Louganis. I love Ricky Martin and Elton John. I love all gay people. I changed. All those religious judgments were lies that only hurt people. All gays, lesbians, bisexuals, transgenders, and queer people deserve the same rights as everyone else."

Kirk and Madsen continued to describe other methods to homosexualize every nation through a campaign of propaganda using eight principles of persuasion (pp. 173-191):

1 – Don't just express yourself: communicate!

2 – Seek ye not the saved nor the damned: appeal to the skeptics

3 – Keep talking

4 – Keep the message focused: you're a homosexual, not a whale

5 – Portray gays as victims, not aggressive challengers

6 – Give potential protectors a just cause

7 – Make gays look good

8 – Make victimizers look bad

Allow me to summarize these eight principles of propaganda so that you may comprehend how well conceived and executed their plan was:

Principle one—"Don't just express yourself, communicate!" Put yourself out there. Share your story. Make heterosexuals believe that you speak their language, look like them, act like them, and dress like them.

Principle two—"Seek ye not the saved nor the damned: appeal to the skeptics." There are "intransigents" that are against homosexuality and made up 30-35% of the population, usually the more religious types. Next are "friends" of homosexuals, who made up 25-30% of the population. Finally, there are "ambivalent skeptics," previously 35-45% of the people. These ambivalent or skeptical people are the primary target of this campaign.

Principle three—"Keep talking." Desensitize and share stories:

"You can forget about trying right up front to persuade folks that homosexuality is a good thing. But if you can get them to think it's just another thing, meriting no more than just a shrug of the shoulders, then your battle for legal and social rights is virtually won" (p. 177).

Keep talking, keep sharing, keep coming out, and let people know you are gay. Regarding religious people with conservative beliefs: "Portray such institutions as antiquated backwaters, badly out of step with the times and with the latest findings of psychology" (p. 179). Talk in public; get on TV, into films, and magazines.

Principle four—"Keep the message focused: you are a homosexual, not a whale." Be single-minded: This is about gay rights; keep talking about gay rights in as many venues as possible, both personally and publicly.

Principle five—"Portray gays as victims, not as aggressive challengers." "The purpose of victim imagery is to make straights feel very uncomfortable; that is, to jam with shame the self-righteous pride that would ordinarily accompany and reward their anti-gay belligerence, and to lay the groundwork for the process of conversion by leading straights to identify with gays and sympathize with their underdog status" (p. 183). Gays are "victims of circumstance" and "victims of prejudice" (p. 184). Help straights become protectors for the victims. "Persons featured in the media campaign should be wholesome and admirable by straight standards and completely unexceptional in all appearance; in other words, they should be indistinguishable from straights we'd like to reach" (p. 183).

> "To suggest in public that homosexuality might be chosen is to open the can of worms labeled 'moral choice and sin' and give the religious intransigents a stick to beat us with. Straights must be taught that it is as natural for some persons to be homosexual as it is for others to be heterosexual: wickedness and seduction have nothing to do with it. And since no choice is involved, gayness can be no more blameworthy than straightness. In fact, it is simply a matter of the odds— one in ten—as to who turns out gay and who straight. Each heterosexual must be led to realize that he might as easily been born homosexual himself" (p. 184).

This is pure genius, normalizing homosexuality, making it equivalent to heterosexuality: according to this concept, you or I could have turned out gay, lesbian, bisexual, transgender, or queer. In Chapter Two I will debunk this false notion.

Misinformation about population percentages was also introduced, creating yet another homosexual myth: "Ten percent of the population is gay." This has no basis in fact or scientific evidence. Although many people change their sexual behavior at various times in their lives, today, according to the latest research studies, it is estimated that perhaps 2-3% of the population live a homosexual life. "About 1.4 percent of the women said they thought of themselves as homosexual or bisexual and about 2.8 percent of the men identified themselves in this way....no matter how we define homosexuality, we come up with small percentages of people who are currently gay or lesbian" (*Sex in America: A Definitive Survey*, Robert T. Michael, John H. Gagnon, Edward O. Laumann, and Gina Kolata, Boston: Little Brown and Co., 1994, pp. 176-177). These results came from surveys conducted by the scholarly team at the University of Chicago, the National Health and Social Life Survey (NHSLS). Kirk and Madsen, along with other homosexual strategists, increased the percentage as yet another strategy to reclassify homosexuality as a substantial "minority" in search of acceptance.

Principle six—"Give potential protectors a just cause." Use anti-discrimination in the campaign against homo-hatred, show how homosexuals are being treated terribly. Anti-discrimination is the calling card.

Principle seven—"Make gays look good." Gays are victims. They are just like everyone else and need our protection. Create television shows and movies with sympathetic LGBTQ+ characters. Make gays look good and have famous people endorse them.

Principle eight—"Make victimizers look bad." Make homo-hating beliefs and actions look so bad that everyone will dissociate from them.

"The best way to make homo-hatred look bad is to vilify those who victimize gays. The public should be shown images of ranting homo-haters whose associated traits and attitudes appall and anger middle America" (p. 189).

The best example I've ever seen of this type of person is Rev. Fred Phelps. He was supposedly a Baptist minister, however, he and his followers preach and practice hate, and they have nothing to do with God and Biblical principles of love (leadership of the Baptist denomination denounced Mr. Phelps). I debated this man on radio many years ago. He is not a godly person. He and his followers attend LGBTQ+ marches and events such as Matthew Shepherd's funeral, carrying signs saying "God hates fags," and "God condemns you to hell." Phelps is a poster boy for homo-hatred. His approach leads members of the LGBTQ+ community to despise people of faith and, to define homosexuals as victims of their hate. Phelps ideally serves the purpose of principle number eight: to make victimizers look bad, creating more sympathy for gay people.

There you have it, the eight principles of propaganda to eliminate prejudice toward LGBTQ+ persons. Finally, the authors introduce three tactics to dominate the media: (1) public relations—keep getting the message out; (2) news reporting—make friends with people in the media, call them, tell them about homosexual-related stories, take them out and befriend them; and (3) advertise—show that LGBTQ+ persons are just like everyone else, and spend time with people in the media. To accomplish this, the authors suggest using television, radio, magazines, newspapers, billboards, and display ads to disseminate their message.

I have been on numerous television shows, i.e., Larry King Live, O'Reilly Factor, 20/20, Jimmy Kimmel Live, CNN, Rachel Maddow Show, etc. Many members of these TV shows' staff (producers, directors, writers, editors, technicians, musicians), as well as the staff of other shows, are active members of the LGBTQ+ community.

They write, produce, and direct the shows, and therefore easily control the message.

The authors' concluding comments explain how to keep the propaganda campaign alive:

> "You may discount what the pious tell you because it is actually rage, not love, that lay behind all those progressive events. Like all emotions, rage has its purpose and its time and its place. When a situation becomes intolerable and oppression unbearable, when millions do not even dare cry out beneath the heel of injustice, rage is the appropriate response" (p. 382).

This sums up Kirk and Madsen's homosexual manifesto. According to them, love will not help to achieve their equal rights. They are calling for continued action: keep your rage burning; we must reverse the engine of prejudice using these tactics.

> The motivation behind the Gay Rights Movement is pain, anger, and rage, which represents wounded souls in desperate need of love and acceptance. This is the fuel that drives their engines: "Accept me. Help me. I'm hurting. Please love me." Again, underneath all their demands are little children looking for love and acceptance.

Capturing the Scientific Community

- Storming the Bastille of the American Psychiatric Association
- Revising Homosexual Diagnosis in the DSM/ICD
- LGBTQ+ Therapists Take Over Mental Health Organizations

Imagine there is a building with a pillar on each side (see the diagram). Let's call this building *The Homosexual Movement*. The pillar on the left side of the building is: "We are born gay." The pillar on the right side of the building is: "We can't change." This is the paradigm that shifted the entire homosexual debate—"born gay and can't change." Here is how they achieved this masterful but false claim through the scientific community in the 1970s.

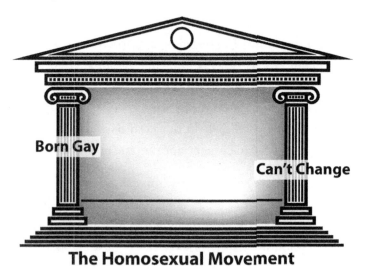

Born Gay   **Can't Change**

The Homosexual Movement

© 2022 Richard A. Cohen, M.A.

Before *After the Ball* was written, other homosexual activists were busy working to influence public opinion. They recognized that the "priests" of the 20th century were no longer religious leaders but members of the medical and mental health professions. If science said it, it must be "truth." LBGTQ+ activists then set out to capture the scientific community in order to promote full acceptance of homosexuality.

From 1970 to 1973 they verbally and emotionally pummeled psychiatrists of the American Psychiatric Association (APA) at their annual conventions. When a psychiatrist presented a paper about the etiology and/or treatment of ego-dystonic homosexuality (someone conflicted over their SSA), LGBTQ+ activists would start screaming, jumping on tables, and shouting, "How dare you treat us like this? How dare you systematize prejudice? You are killing us.

Stop killing us!" While they were screaming, they filled their tirades with obscenities.

They ripped open their chests and exposed their hearts: "We're mad as hell and we're not going to take it anymore! Stop discriminating against us!" Their pain was palpable; however, they used it as a ploy to *force* psychiatrists to remove homosexuality as an illness from the Diagnostic and Statistical Manual of Mental Disorders (DSM). The DSM is the "bible" of diagnostic disorders that therapists and physicians use throughout the USA. (Most therapists and physicians worldwide use the International Classification of Diseases, known as the ICD).

Homosexual activists within and outside the APA started a letter-writing campaign to all the voting membership, imploring them to remove the diagnosis of homosexuality from the DSM. The National Gay and Lesbian Task Force funded this effort, as documented in Dr. Ronald Bayer's book, *Homosexuality and American Psychiatry*. Ronald Bayer, professor at Columbia University, was previously at the Hastings Center, a research institute devoted to the study of ethical issues in medicine and the life sciences. Members of the APA had no idea who was behind this letter writing campaign. A scientific issue became politicized overnight, part of the strategy employed by key LGBTQ+ activists.

In December of 1973, by a narrow vote, homosexuality was removed from the DSM. The vote was not based on scientific research but on political pressure from LGBTQ+ activists. Dr. Bayer wrote,

"Instead of being engaged in a sober consideration of data, psychiatrists were swept up in a political controversy. The American Psychiatric Association had fallen victim to the disorder of a tumultuous year, when disruptive conflicts threatened to politicize every aspect of American social life… The result was not a conclusion based on an approximation of the scientific truth as dictated by reason, but was instead an action demanded by the ideological temper of the time" (*Homosexuality and American Psychiatry*, Ronald Bayer, Princeton University Press, Princeton, NJ, 1981, pp. 3-4).

Following the narrow vote to remove homosexuality from the DSM, newspapers worldwide reported, "Doctors declare homosexuality normal," even though that was not said by the APA psychiatrists. That is how gay activists spun this decision. It was a coup d'état. The APA was kidnapped by LGBTQ+ activists.

Science went out the window and politics came in the door. Since that time therapists were discouraged from discussing the potential causes and successful treatment of unwanted same-sex attraction in any mental health organization, including the American Psychiatric Association, American Psychological Association, American Counseling Association, American Medical Association, and all other professional organizations. They all drank the Kool-Aid.

Those professionals who offer research on the etiology and treatment of unwanted same-sex attraction are labeled "homophobic," "anti-gay," and publicly humiliated—so much for "tolerance, diversity, and equality," the mantra of the Gay Rights Movement. In fact, true tolerance is a two-way street where diverse opinions are heard and respected. The decision by the APA in December of 1973 created a new mentality regarding homosexuality in the mental health profession: If it isn't broke, then we don't need to fix it. However, it took more than a decade for other countries to adopt the same position and remove the diagnosis of homosexuality from the ICD.

Dr. Robert Spitzer, former professor of psychiatry at Columbia University, was a key player in this whole APA phenomenon that took place in the early 1970s. He was the chair of the nomenclature committee that was investigating whether or not to remove the diagnosis of homosexuality from the DSM. After much debate, he advised them to remove it. Now fast-forward thirty years later: in October 2003, Dr. Spitzer published a study in the *Archives of Sexual Behavior* about 200 men and women who changed from a homosexual to a heterosexual orientation. He acknowledged that these changes had, in fact, taken place. Can you imagine the outrage of homosexual activists? Dr. Spitzer received hate mail, threatening phone calls, and others tried to have him fired from his position as professor of psychiatry at Columbia University. He wrote an Op Ed piece for the *Wall Street Journal* essentially saying, 'Ladies and gentlemen, we are scientists and have the right to investigate phenomena. Let's cut the politics. We have a scientific obligation to discuss all issues.' However, in 2013 Spitzer caved into the political pressure by LGBTQ+ activists and wrote an apology for his study in The New York Times. However, this public apology did not invalidate the findings of his study as he asked the *Archives of Sexual Behavior* to remove his study but they refused saying it was scientifically valid. I was one of the participants in his study, as well as a dozen of my former clients. Additionally, I know approximately one hundred of the participants who are all living happy, heterosexual lives.

Today almost all mental health organizations promote what is called "gay affirmative therapy." In undergraduate and graduate psychology courses, there is rarely a discussion about the etiology and/or treatment of unwanted SSA. Students in counseling programs are taught gay affirmative therapy, hardly aware of the possibility of change. In some universities, psychology students have been expelled from their program because they refused to counsel gay identified clients or couples based on their religious beliefs. In other states and countries, teachers were fired because they would not affirm homosexual behavior based upon their spiritual convictions. To cite one example, Julea Ward was expelled from her graduate counseling program at Eastern Michigan University in March 2009, because she said that she was unable to counsel a homosexual couple because of her religious beliefs. This is just one example of reverse discrimination.

When a client comes in for treatment and experiences unwanted homosexual feelings, or does not want to accept his or her homosexuality, the new diagnosis is "internalized homophobia." The majority of trained professional therapists today instruct all SSA clients to accept themselves as gay, without a mention about the possibility of change. If the parents and family members do not accept their child's or sibling's homosexuality, they are shamed. They too are classified as having "internalized homophobia." The parents, family members, or friends who cannot accept their loved ones homosexual identity or behavior are considered part of the problem, and they are shamed into changing their views.

The American Psychological Association in 2007 created a task force to study sexual reorientation therapies that help those who experience unwanted SSA fulfill their heterosexual potential. This committee consisted of strictly gay-identified therapists and those who support homosexuality. The APA refused to allow any sexual reorientation therapists on their task force. Their results were predictable: this type of therapy is contra-indicated. In other words, it doesn't really work. But if one carefully reads their results, they stated that the studies showing change were not rigorously conducted. That means they are not sure if this type of therapy works. So much for the client's right of self-determination. Again, politics trumped science.

Religious Institutions Revise Theology: Historical Relativism

- Historical Relativism, Revisionist or Pro-Gay Theology
- Religions Divided Down the Middle
- Para-Church Ministries Reach Out to Those Who Experience Unwanted SSA

In today's religious community, there is a great divide over homosexuality:

Side one: "Homosexuality is sinful, it's an abomination. We reject homosexual people and their behavior."

Side two: "Homosexuals are wonderful! We endorse their homosexual identity and homosexual behavior."

Proponents of homosexuality within the religious community have reinvented theology. Their position is called "historical relativism," and/or "revisionist/pro-gay theology." Gay theology is based on three principles: 1) many past Biblical prohibitions are no longer valid today, 2) Scriptures regarding homosexual behavior did not include committed gay couples, and 3) authors of the Bible did not have the latest scientific facts, that people are born gay. These principles are the basis for Gay Theology.

The two polar attitudes—endorsing and condemning homosexuality—miss the mark entirely. We need a paradigm shift, a centrist view that states:

> "If you experience SSA, God loves you and we love you too. You are welcome here. We do not approve of any sexual behavior outside of marriage between a man and a woman. We believe that you were not essentially born with same-sex attraction. God loves you, and so do we. We embrace all people. You are welcome in our synagogue, in our church, in our mosque, in our temple."

We need to be protectors of those who experience SSA and offer them unconditional love along with truth and healing. We need to separate the person from their behavior. Scripture does not speak negatively about people who experience SSA in either the Old or New Testament. All Scriptures refer to homosexual behavior, as well as heterosexual behavior outside of marriage. There is no condemnation for people who experience SSA.

Most religious denominations are divided straight down the middle when it comes to the homosexual issue, debating whether or not to ordain active homosexual clergy and/or marry homosexual couples. These two divisive issues confront every religion worldwide, wreaking havoc and shattering peoples' faith. "Did God make people gay?" "Are they truly born this way?" "Should we revisit and revise what the Bible (and other religious teachings) actually says about homosexual behavior being sinful?" LGBTQ+ persons are challenging all traditional faith understandings of homosexuality. Episcopalians, Anglicans, Lutherans, Methodists, Presbyterians, Catholics, Baptists, Mormons, Jews, Hindus, and other faiths are equally divided on this issue. Muslims still disapprove of homosexual behavior, although it is quietly practiced in all Islamic countries. There are more and more Muslim LGBTQ+ activists trying to change their customs and culture.

Although many denominational doctrines promote a Biblical view of sexuality—marriage is meant to be only between a man and a woman and all sex outside of marriage is incompatible with God's design for human sexuality—they are daily conforming to the changing social trend of accepting homosexuality and incorporating those beliefs into church and/or religious doctrine. Revisionist Theology is the fashion of the day—old ways are not applicable to new understandings, therefore, we must yield to a more modern view.

Many religions have two para-church organizations:

(1) LGBTQ+ groups which endorse homosexual behavior.

(2) Groups that assist men and women who experience unwanted SSA.

Catholic: Dignity (pro-homosexual) vs. Courage (healing homosexuality)

Episcopal: Integrity (pro-homosexual) vs. none

Methodist: Reconciling Ministries (pro-homosexual) vs. Transforming Congregations (healing homosexuality)

Presbyterian: More Light Presbyterians / Covenant Network of Presbyterians (pro-homosexual) vs. One By One (healing homosexuality)

Mormon: Affirmation (pro-homosexual) vs. North Star (healing homosexuality)

Jewish: Many pro-homosexual Jewish groups vs. none at this time (a New Jersey court prohibited a Jewish organization from helping those who experience unwanted SSA).

Historically most people of faith treated same-sex attracted men and women abominably. Now, instead of repenting to these men and women on bended knees, many religious faiths are throwing the baby out with the bathwater—revising theology without truly understanding what drives homosexual behavior. Instead of learning more about same-sex attraction, they are succumbing to political pressure and following social trends by endorsing homosexual behavior. Everyone is losing. Although members of the LGBTQ+ community think they are finally getting what they want, will this tactic truly give them they need?

Media and Entertainment Industry Promote Homosexuality

- Television Shows Created By LGBTQ+ persons
- Movies: LGBTQ+ Moguls Rule Hollywood
- News and Cable Shows with Pro-Homosexual Views

Years ago my wife and I were guests on the Montel Williams Show (a popular talk show at the time). An openly gay staff member met us at the train station. I asked him, "Do you know why we are here?" He said, "Oh yes, and I have contacted members of LGBTQ+ groups in both New York City and New Jersey to be in the audience." It turned out that the show was an ambush, meant to denigrate me as well as the other guests who spoke a loving message about the possibility of coming out of homosexuality.

This experience has become the daily diet for those of us who promote the possibility of changing from same-sex attracted to opposite-sex attracted. Over the past thirty-five years I have been on countless TV shows, done hundreds of radio interviews, and have been written about in newspapers and magazines worldwide. I have seen the power of gays in the media, mostly behind the scenes, setting the agenda for national dialogue. In 2000, when I released my first book, *Coming Out Straight: Understanding and Healing Homosexuality* (rewritten and released as *Being Gay: Nature, Nurture or Both?* in 2020), I hired a publicist to help promote the book. I hired her because she was "gay-affirming" and no one in the media would accuse me of being anti-gay. She had connections with all the major TV shows in the USA. She was confident that she would garner interviews for me on the most important morning and prime time talk shows.

She soon found one door after another closing in her face! "Richard, I have tried my best. I have to say in all honesty, I was the bigot. At first, I thought that I could not work with you because you were anti-gay. But, actually, I was the one who was prejudiced, and not you. I experience you as a loving, caring, and genuinely compassionate man." She continued, "I was dumbfounded that the so-called 'liberal media' is so intolerant! They are completely closed to your view. I have done my best and failed. I'm sorry."

Each year at the Oscars, Golden Globes, and Emmys Awards, which are broadcast on television worldwide, we see many gay, lesbian, and now trans actors accept awards. They kiss their partners; they publicly thank their partners, and many allude to the glories of being gay and the need for more acceptance. This is just another means of normalizing homosexual behavior and gaining public acceptance.

Again we return to the Homosexual Manifesto's commission to members of the LGBTQ+ community: "Tell your stories to the media, say them loud and clear, be convincing, be a victim and gain straight people's support." This has been accomplished. Many in the LGBTQ+ community hold powerful positions in Hollywood and in the media.

Television:

> *Grey's Anatomy, Big Sky, How to Get Away with Murder, Queer as Folk, Modern Family, Glee, Hollywood,* and *Looking* are just a few television shows with LGBTQ+ lead characters. Over the past three decades more and more gay characters have been introduced into everyday life, thus creating more acceptance and the normalcy of homosexuality.

At the beginning of all Dreamworks films is their trademark, a little boy sitting on the moon fishing. Below are the initials SKG, which stand for Steven Spielberg, Jeffrey Katzenberg, and David Geffen.

Mr. Geffen (with an estimated net worth of almost five billion dollars) is a record executive, film and theatrical producer. As a gay man, he has tremendous power and influence in Hollywood and politics. He has donated millions of dollars to various political campaigns as well as to HRC and other homosexual organizations (more about HRC and other homosexual political groups later).

Geffen serves as just one example of innumerable LGBTQ+ persons in powerful positions, who are crafting their message for an unsuspecting public. Ryan Murphy is another major Hollywood writer, producer, and director. There are many people in front of and behind the camera on television and films that are framing the debate and discussion about homosexuality—"gay is good," "those who seek change or promote this opportunity are bad," and "those who do not fully accept homosexuality are 'homophobic,' 'anti-gay,' ignorant people." Most movies and television shows sympathetically portray LGBTQ+ men and women and demonize anyone who disagrees with their behavior.

Educational System Endorses Gay Identity and Relationships

- Gay Straight Alliance (GSA) in Public Schools
- Gay Lesbian Straight Education Network (GLSEN)
- Health Curricula Revised: "Born Gay and Cannot Change"

Many years ago, in my eldest son's high school, there was a Gay Straight Alliance (GSA). A GSA club enters public and private schools under the guise of protecting LGBTQ+ students, and very quickly turns to the promotion of homosexuality. These groups impugn the integrity of anyone who disagrees with their beliefs. I saw this firsthand in my son's high school. Any student who has a different viewpoint about homosexual behavior, based on religious, spiritual, or psychological views, is called names and discriminated against. Where is the tolerance? Where is the diversity of opinion? Where is the equality?

There are thousands of GSAs in middle and high schools across the USA and around the world, initiated by the Gay Lesbian Straight Education Network (GLSEN) founded by Kevin Jennings in 1990. Kevin's autobiography, *Mamma's Boy, Preacher's Son*, recounts his horrific experiences from elementary through high school, being ridiculed and mocked by fellow students while being unprotected by teachers and school administrators. I will share an evaluation of why I believe Kevin Jennings experiences SSA in Chapter Three. From 2009 – 2011, he served as the Assistant Deputy Secretary for Safe and Drug-Free Schools under the U.S. Department of Education in the Obama administration. He was essentially the "Safe School Czar," dictating public policy and protecting LGBTQ+ students from being bullied. He attempted to heal the hurt that he and so many other gay children experienced when they were in school. But while he may be creating a safer environment for them, he was at the same time betraying the very essence of their true gender identity. More about this later.

Mission of GLSEN: "Championing LGBTQ+ issues in K-12 education since 1990 GLSEN works to ensure that LGBTQ+ students are able to learn and grow in a school environment free from bullying and harassment. Together we can transform our nation's schools into the safe and affirming environment all youth deserve" (https://www.glsen.org). "Today, after over 25 years of leading the movement, GLSEN's national network is more than 1.5 million strong, with students, families, educators, and education advocates working to create safe schools. More than 500,000 GLSEN resources are downloaded by students and educators each year" (https://www.glsen.org/about-us). GLSEN believes in respect for those who agree with them, but treats those with differing views as hostile and unacceptable, calling them derogatory names.

Children's books like *Heather Has Two Mommies*, *Daddy's Roommate*, and *Gloria Goes to Gay Pride* are just a few examples of how children in elementary school are being enrolled into believing the homosexual myth. Movies such as *It's Elementary* (shown in public and private schools around the nation and on television) are also soliciting children into this false ideology. Sensitivity trainings for schoolteachers further their cause. Most school libraries carry books promoting homosexual behavior while completely ignoring the reality that there is another side to this issue.

Health curricula taught to elementary, middle, and high school students in many communities throughout the country and world also include teaching on homosexuality—basically, people are born gay and cannot change. I saw this first hand in my younger son's health classes when he was in middle school. These curricula are *not* scientifically valid, yet they are being used to propagandize future generations with false information about homosexuality (desensitize, jam, convert). If they remain unchallenged, our children will become puppets of a propaganda machine as well as future voters, endorsing homosexual behavior because they know nothing other than the homosexual myth: born gay and cannot change.

Political Pressure to Enact Homosexual Legislation

- Human Rights Campaign (HRC)
- Lambda Legal
- Parents and Friends of Lesbians and Gays (PFLAG)
- National Gay and Lesbian Task Force
- Gay and Lesbian Alliance Against Defamation (GLADD)

> Members of LGBTQ+ organizations are driven by their hurt, pain, and a need for belonging, acceptance, and love. Homosexual organizations founded in the USA fund and educate homosexual groups worldwide. They have taught and continue to mentor new organizations about how to achieve acceptance in the fields of science, religion, education, media, entertainment, and politics.

The world's largest LGBTQ+ *political action committee* is the **Human Rights Campaign (HRC)**. Their annual budget is well over a $44 million (as of 2022). They have a national headquarters building located at DuPont Circle in the heart of Washington, D.C., with a full-time staff of over 100, and thousands of volunteers around the USA and in many countries throughout the world. They work in the political arena for "gay rights legislation" (www.hrc.org), to enact homosexual legislation on the federal, state and local levels.

Many years ago I spoke at a church in St. Paul, Minnesota. Over 300 people attended. About one-third of the audience was either gay identified or were LGBTQ+ activists, many of whom wore apparel from the Human Rights Campaign (they have a recognizable logo with a blue background and yellow equals stripes in the middle). To say that the HRC representatives were upset when I shared my belief, that people are not essentially born with SSA and that changing from same-sex attracted to opposite-sex attracted is possible, would be an understatement. This is so because their lives are predicated upon the innate, immutable paradigm—*born with SSA, cannot change.*

During the question and answer session following the talk, many wanted my head on a chopping block. Instead, I offered them love and compassion, agreeing to disagree, showing them the face of true tolerance and real diversity. *Love is the greatest medicine to heal all pain.*

HRC is active and on the move from city to city, state to state, and government to government. I have debated several HRC staff members on various television and radio interviews. They are polished and professional, showing a pleasant and amiable face to homosexuality, as taught to them in the Homosexual Manifesto. They work tirelessly to transform legislation to incorporate homosexual behavior into every city, state, and federal law. Be aware, changes are happening daily unbeknownst to most of us.

Lambda Legal is a litigious organization that challenges and sues state, federal, and other country's laws pertaining to homosexual behavior, as well as supporting other homosexual activities worldwide (lambdalegal.org). Most LGBTQ+ legal victories within the USA have either been won in the courts or through legislation, and more recently through popular vote. HRC influences legislators while Lambda Legal works within the court system. The Supreme Court of the U.S.A. enacted homosexual marriage in June 2015.

Parents and Friends of Lesbians and Gays (PFLAG) at www. pflag.org, promotes homosexuality throughout the country. They have over 400 chapters in 50 states with over 325,000 members and supporters. PFLAG vision: "Our Mission: To create a caring, just, and affirming world for LGBTQ+ people and those who love them. Our Vision: An equitable, inclusive world where every LGBTQ+ person is safe, celebrated, empowered, and loved" (https://pflag.org/mission).

I found this a bit contradictory since I have participated in several PFLAG meetings, at which I was mocked and ridiculed for my personal beliefs about homosexuality that no one is born this way and change is possible. My colleagues and I have discovered that tolerance from LGBTQ+ organizations goes something like this: "My way or the highway!" PFLAG members visit public schools under the guise of non-discrimination, and promote total acceptance of homosexuality with total disregard for other views. They are wonderful and good-hearted people who are simply ignorant about the facts of SSA.

Other significant and powerful homosexual organizations:

National Gay and Lesbian Task Force (www.thetaskforce.org): "The mission of the National Gay and Lesbian Task Force is to build the grassroots power of the lesbian, gay, bisexual and transgender (LGBTQ+) community. We do this by training activists, equipping state and local organizations with the skills needed to organize broad-based campaigns to defeat anti-LGBTQ+ referenda and advance pro-LGBTQ+ legislation, and building the organizational capacity of our movement. Our Policy Institute, the movement's premier think tank, provides research and policy analysis to support the struggle for complete equality and to counter right-wing lies. As part of a broader social justice movement, we work to create a nation that respects the diversity of human expression and identity and creates opportunity for all" (http://www.thetaskforce.org/about_us/mission_statements).

Gay and Lesbian Alliance Against Defamation (GLAAD at glaad.org): "The Gay & Lesbian Alliance Against Defamation (GLAAD) is dedicated to promoting and ensuring fair, accurate and inclusive representation of people and events in the media as a means of eliminating homophobia and discrimination based on gender identity and sexual orientation" (http://www.glaad.org/mission). GLAAD activists serve as media watchdogs and come down hard on anyone who does not agree with promoting homosexuality. Yes, protection is necessary, but they don't provide the whole picture. In their perspective, no other opinion is allowed to be heard on this issue. After I participated in an interview on CNN in April 2010, GLADD attacked CNN for allowing me to share my viewpoint. In fact, the majority of coverage on CNN, along with most other cable and network television news, promotes only homosexual views. Again, where is the diversity? Where is their tolerance? What about equality?

Apart from these non-governmental agencies stands the most powerful entity of all—the US Government. "As of April 29, 2021–the 100 Days mark of Joe Biden's presidency–over 200 known LGBTQ+ people have been appointed to his administration, the most in history at this point in any administration" (https://victoryinstitute.org/programs/presidential-appointments-initiative/LGBTQ+-appointments-in-the-biden-harris-administration).

Conclusion

As I re-read this chapter, which briefly traces the history of the homosexual movement, pain gripped my heart. How sad and unjust are the terrible ways that same-sex attracted men and women have been treated throughout history so often by their families, in their places of worship, in their schools, and in their neighborhoods. My heart breaks for each one of them, because I used to be like them. And yet, I know by pursuing acceptance through revisionist theology, compromised science, media spin, and special legislation, they will never experience the love and peace they so desperately seek and deserve.

> *The goal of this book is to promote real change and true love for all who experience SSA, so they may find warm and welcoming places in their families, places of worship, workplaces, and communities.*

Who or what is the real enemy of the LGBTQ+ community? Is it a person or people? Is it parents who cannot endorse their child's homosexual behavior? Is it religious institutions that still hold sacred traditional Biblical or Koranic principles? Is it a therapist who helps those who experience unwanted SSA? No. *The real enemy is ignorance and fear.* Because of very real discrimination, LGBTQ+ activists created a brilliant strategic plan to gain acceptance. Yet this plan was based on a false paradigm to persuade people that they were born gay, cannot change, and therefore everyone must love and accept them just as they are. This paradigm has worked, but the biggest losers are the men and women who may get what they think they want but will be denied what they truly need.

In summary, laws are being challenged and changed daily. Homosexual marriage laws are marching from country to country. The educational system has become more tolerant and sensitive to LGBTQ+ students while falsely teaching pro-homosexual lessons through health education curricula. Religious institutions continue to revise their faith traditions in order to accommodate gay identified men and women. Media and movies are basically the sound stage to promote homosexuality unchallenged, without debate. Scientific organizations are reluctant to allow any discussion about the causes and treatment of unwanted same-sex attraction.

We can and must reverse this through education and understanding. Allow me to offer a new perspective about homosexuality—where it actually originates. But first, let's hear from someone who experienced unwanted SSA and made a remarkable transformation to being married with kids! In his own words, please enjoy Joseph's story.

Joseph's Story

In this book, I am including stories of three men and one woman who came out of homosexuality. My intention is to help you better understand the meaning behind same-sex attraction and to offer an understanding about how to assist those who desire to change. After each story, I will describe why I believe the writer experienced SSA. I'll also suggest how family and friends might help such individuals discover their innate heterosexual potential. Through this I hope you will acquire practical ideas how to assist anyone who experiences SSA, whether they wish to change or not. Learning to love the right ways will help all who experience SSA.

First is Joseph's story. He was my client for two years.

I was born in Europe. I lived there for more than twenty years. Thinking back always brings to mind the image of not having a particularly happy childhood. I was a very sensitive child, and so the confrontation with reality was much more difficult for me than it was for others. I can't tell exactly when I started to feel attractions towards boys. Several years ago I realized that my uncle sexually abused me. I spent much time with him when I was three to five years old. When I first retrieved those memories, I felt terrified to remember the actual events. What were more painful and intense were the feelings connected with the abuse, all the feelings that were stored in my body and mind for so many years. During my therapy I virtually re-experienced the feelings that I had as a boy. Believe it or not, I am very happy to have recovered those memories, to know about it, because it is one factor that led to my homosexual desires.

My mother was at home with my brother and me. When I was a toddler, she did not give me the opportunity to break away from her and find my own way. I was educated to be the good boy. My father worked a lot and was seldom home; therefore no one was around to balance my mother's role in my life. My brother was born when I was nine years old. From the time of his birth, I was very jealous because I felt that he was the main focus of the family.

Growing up as a teenager was a good time for me because I had lots of friends in school, but at home I was still unhappy. My friends became my family, and I had sexual encounters with some of my male friends. Mutual masturbation and oral sex were the things we did together, and I started to like it. Around the same time, I found my father's pornographic magazines, and masturbation became more and more like a friend in my lonely life at home.

I never understood why I felt attractions towards boys and men. I felt it was one of the biggest burdens in my life because I also liked being with women, and I definitely wanted to have a family. After finishing high school, my life became even more confused. A good friend of mine went into the gay lifestyle. I didn't know if I should do the same.

At the same time, I was in love with a girl that somehow protected me. I still felt confused, but a trip to the U.S.A. helped to clarify my life and dreams. During the visit, I stayed with a gay couple. Through spending time with them, I realized that the gay lifestyle was absolutely *not* right for me. This helped define my dreams, but I still felt attractions towards men. In a way, it was more difficult now because I knew for sure that I did not want to live a gay life.

At that time, I started to act out. I had sex with men in public parks and bathrooms. Even though it did not happen so often, it still gave me the feeling that I could meet my need for intimacy with men. It did not take too long before realizing how terrible the whole situation was. I tried to stay away from acting out as often as I could. I was partially successful because I relied more on masturbation, using gay pornography to repress my need for male intimacy.

At this time, I was studying at a university. A friend helped me a lot. Through her, I heard about a therapist who specialized in helping people who experienced unwanted homosexual feelings. I finally met him during one of his seminar tours through Europe in 1994. For the first time in my life, I talked to someone about my problems and homosexual desires. Richard Cohen was very understanding and helpful. He explained to me the root causes of this condition. He told me that there was the possibility of healing. At that point, I had hope again. God, who helped me to get through all those painful years, had given me a wonderful gift!

My plan was to go to America and receive therapy. A year after I met Richard in Europe, I came to the U.S.A. There I went into therapy with a colleague of his. It was great because, for the first time, I could really share my story. I felt understood and not alone for the first time in my life.

After a couple of months in the States, I had to return to Europe to finish school. I also started to prepare to return for a longer period of time to receive more therapy and join a support group. Back at home, I had wonderful friends who totally supported me and especially a close friend of mine who knew my story, and he literally was there for me whenever I needed him. He held me and we played sports together. We had fun and worked on different projects at our college campus.

At the time, I also met my wife-to-be, and I told her from the very beginning about my homosexual attractions. She said, "We will master it together!" She accompanied me back to the States. I began therapy with Richard and joined his support group. I also found a healing partner, which helped a lot. It was sometimes rough, but I learned more and more about myself. I discovered my inner child through various techniques that Richard taught me. This helped incredibly to heal the wounds of my past. Additionally, I used bioenergetics to release a lot of anger and pain stored in my body and soul.

Today, I have come a long way. Quite infrequently I experience attractions towards men. I learned it is just an indication that I am not caring for myself properly. When I address the issue, the attractions go away instantly. I feel very good, and I see that I grow closer to my wife every day. I am grateful to God to have had this opportunity to heal. I am grateful to those who pioneered this way of resolving unwanted homosexual feelings.

Comments

I worked with Joseph for two years. He made tremendous progress in that time. One of the most important parts of his therapy was learning about his inner child (inner child is another name for the unconscious). Joseph not only had problems with compulsive masturbation and anonymous sexual behavior, he also had an eating disorder. Food and sex were his way of medicating his pain. Food and sex were love to him.

When he did the inner child workbook, he discovered a whole new world. Because of his devotion to his healing work, the voice within began to disclose more and more about his past and present situation. Joseph became a good parent to his inner family. The more he listened, the more he learned. Because of this and his healing relationships with other men, the homosexual desires naturally dissipated.

Joseph also had to learn a marvelous new word, which had not been a part of his vocabulary in either English or his native tongue. That word was "No." As he stated, he grew up being a "good boy" for his mommy and others. In his recovery work, he did a lot of bioenergetics to reawaken his masculine energy. When he finally got the hang of it, Joseph cut loose, and oceans of rage and pain were released. The support group was of tremendous benefit to him. Also, he was a gift to the group, as he readily shared himself with others. In this way, he mentored the newcomers.

Toward the end of our therapeutic relationship, Joseph invited his entire family over to America for a family healing session. It lasted one day, and it was simply magnificent. He was able to share with his mom and tell her how much pain he experienced by her overprotective nature. They wept together. She apologized, not realizing what she had done hurt her son so deeply.

He held his father, crying the tears of a child who so longed for his father's affection and attention. He told his dad how much he missed him when he was out working and in the pubs at night with his friends. "Why didn't you ever take me with you to work?" They, too, wept. His father apologized, and finally Joseph felt his strong daddy's arms around him. Now, their relationship is deepening with each visit. Joseph has requested that his mother back off for now so that he and his dad can bond.

Another amazing event took place during the family healing session. Joseph was able to apologize to his younger brother for the abusive way that he had treated him because of the intense jealousy he experienced. His brother expressed his pain, screaming about what he had gone through. They held each other, grieving together and reconnected in heart. Finally, his younger brother shared with Mom and Dad how their fighting hurt him. The entire family held each other, all in tears, releasing years of unexpressed pain. It was a new beginning for this family. Today, Joseph is more and more in love with his wife. Their sex life is great, his same-sex desires are gone, and they have three beautiful children. Joseph has now become a mentor and coach for men who experience unwanted same-sex attraction.

Conclusion

As you read Joseph's story, were you able to understand some of the reasons why he experienced SSA? In the next chapter, I will give a more detailed explanation of what contributes to the development of same-sex attraction in men and women. Here's a quick overview of Joseph's challenges:

1. Joseph experienced insufficient bonding with his father, and therefore was unable to incorporate his dad's masculinity and feel his own maleness. A boy first gets his sense of gender identity from his father. Joseph missed this important stage of psychosexual development.
2. Joseph was overly attached to his mother, internalizing her femininity. Many SSA boys were too close to their moms and too distant from their dads. This precludes them from

experiencing their own masculine gender identity. Instead, they over-identify with women and/or the feminine.

3. Joseph, along with many boys and girls who experience SSA, was highly sensitive, or hypersensitive. This temperament led to his acute feelings of being rejected by his father and being different from others.

4. Joseph developed the habit of acting like a pleaser. Many, who experience SSA, because they are hypersensitive, use their talents and gifts to win people's love. Joseph worked to obtain good grades, and to be an excellent student.

5. Joseph experienced sexual abuse by his uncle when he was three-to-five years old. This created a neurological pattern equating male sexual behavior with receiving love and attention. Joseph's father was absent from his life, so the relationship with his uncle became a substitute for male attention.

6. In puberty, the normal needs for pre-adolescent male bonding became sexualized. At first Joseph resisted and felt guilty. However, there was hole in his soul, a normal need to belong to the world of men, and sex became his substitute for healthy male bonding. The pattern of anonymous sex in Joseph's life served several purposes: (1) here Joseph showed up as real, no longer the "good boy," but rather getting down and dirty, something he never allowed himself to be in real life, a powerful man, and (2) he used sex to experience some form of connection with men, that which was lacking in his early years of child development, being disconnected from his father.

Suggestions

Once we understand the dynamics that can lead to SSA, we may develop a list of ways family and friends can help:

1. Fathers, bond with your sons. Mothers, bond with your daughters. A child experiences the fullness of his or her own

gender identity by successfully internalizing their same-sex parent's love. Even if your child has a different type of personality or temperament, it is still essential that they bond with you, and thereby incorporate either your maleness or femaleness. You are the primary source of gender identity for your son or daughter. Therefore, join in their world first, understand how they experience life, and then you may bring them into your world. Dads, do activities with yours sons, and moms, do things with your daughters. Keep it in mind that kids who are most likely to develop SSA are hypersensitive, and therefore will easily withdraw. Pursue them with unconditional love.

2. Guys, embrace other guys. Women, embrace other women. The second source from which we gain a sense of our gender identity in pre-adolescence is through hanging out with and connecting to those of our same sex—guys with guys, and girls with girls. If this doesn't happen in those formative years of development, then people who acquire same-sex attraction may spend the rest of their lives looking for that sense of connection through homosexual relationships. However, the original need is that of a child and/or pre-adolescent, to feel a sense of belonging with those of the same sex.

3. In this case, Joseph needed male mentors to embrace him, to introduce him into the world of men. He experienced sexual abuse at an early age. The pattern of sexualizing relationships with men developed due to the lack of bonding with his father. The antidote to this is having male mentors and friends reach out to the hypersensitive boys, showing them healthy male affection and acceptance, teaching them the ways of men. This will save these sensitive souls from a lifetime of seeking love through sexual activities.

4. Oftentimes, when a man who experiences SSA gets into a close relationship with a healthy, heterosexual men, his homosexual

feelings may temporarily subside. However, deep in his heart are the wounds that created those desires in the first place, and they will eventually need to be addressed and resolved. The natural process of healing is grieving the losses of one's past. What was created in unhealthy relationships needs to be healed in healthy relationships. Therefore, allow the SSA man to release his anger, hurt, and pain from past relationships— hurts like the lack of father-son connection, sexual abuse, rejection by male peers, and over-attachment with mother. When the heart is heard and healed, then one's SSA will wane and opposite-sex desires are able to naturally arise.

Chapter Two

Homosexuality:
Nature, Nurture or Both?

Are people born Gay? Are homosexual feelings the result of genes, hormones, or biological differences? In this chapter we will compare the homosexual myth—"*born gay and cannot change*"—with scientific research and theory. What you will come to understand is that SSA is the result of three things:

(1) Innate temperament
(2) Wounds that haven't healed
(3) Unmet needs for love

As we have learned, LGBTQ+ activists spent decades and numerous resources promoting the homosexual myth. Trying to turn the wheel of propaganda is not easy, but facts are facts and the truth will ultimately prevail.

In the world today, there are two views regarding homosexuality: 1) the essentialist claims that people are born this way, while 2) the constructionist says it is basically an acquired condition. We know that SSA is a bio-psycho-social phenomenon. Anyone claiming that people are simply "born gay" is misleading you by spinning inconclusive and faulty research.

Potential Variables
Creating Same-Sex Attraction

Heredity
- Inherited wounds
- Unresolved family issues
- Misperceptions
- Mental filters
- Predilection for rejection

Temperament
- Hypersensitive
- High maintenance
- Artistic nature
- Gender-nonconforming behaviors: Male more feminine; Female more masculine

Hetero-Emotional Wounds
- Enmeshment
- Neglect
- Abuse
- Abandonment
- Addictions
- Imitations of behaviors
- Wrong sex

Homo-Emotional Wounds
- Neglect
- Abuse
- Enmeshment
- Abandonment
- Addictions
- Imitations of behaviors
- Wrong sex

Sibling Wounds / Family Dynamics
- Put-downs
- Abuse
- Name calling

Body-Image Wounds
- Late bloomer
- Physical disabilities
- Shorter
- Thinner
- Larger
- Lack of coordination

Sexual Abuse
- Homosexual imprinting
- Learned and reinforced behaviors
- Substitute for affection

Social or Peer Wounds
- Name calling
- Put-downs
- Goody-goody
- Teacher's pet
- Non-athletic
- No rough and-tumble (boy)
- Too rough and-tumble (girl)

Cultural Wounds
- Media
- Educational system
- Entertainment industry
- Internet
- Pornography

Other Factors
- Divorce
- Death
- Intrauterine experiences & influences
- Adoption
- Religion

The severity of wounding in each category will have a direct impact on the amount of time and effort it will take to heal.

© Richard Cohen, M.A., 2022

Over the past decades, many homosexual researchers have tried to prove that people are born with SSA. Their data is inconclusive, has not been replicated, and in most cases is easy to debunk. If you wish a more detailed scientific evaluation of why people are *not* born with SSA, please read *My Genes Made Me Do It!*, by Dr. Neil and Briar Whitehead (free download available at www.mygenes.co.nz).

Previously, the American Psychological Association (APA) said that homosexuality was inherently innate. However, in 2008 they finally relented and agreed with what the scientific research really showed:

"Although much research has examined the possible genetic, hormonal, developmental, social, and cultural influences on sexual orientation, no findings have emerged that permit scientists to conclude that sexual orientation is determined by any particular factor or factors" (http://www.apa.org/topics/sorientation.html).

In this chapter, we will explore:
- Biological and Genetic Studies about SSA
- Hidden Meaning Behind SSA
- Ten Potential Causes of SSA
- Seven Stages of "Coming Out"
- Resolving Unwanted SSA *is* Possible

Biological and Genetic Studies about SSA

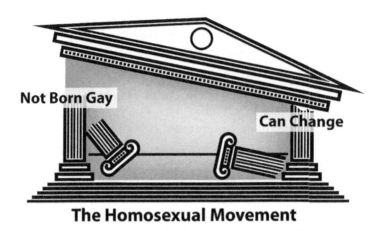

© 2022 Richard A. Cohen, M.A.

While studies, which try to purport a genetic, biologic, or hormonal basis for SSA, continue to emerge, no simple explanation will materialize because our sexuality is influenced by many factors. As we will learn, SSA develops throughout childhood and early adolescence, when the individual's brain and character have yet to reach full maturity. This is one explanation of why we may see the brains of those with SSA not fully actualized with their own gender identity. Also, through scientific studies, we know that the structure of the brain and chemistry of the body are changed by repeated behaviors. Therefore, in many studies, rather than observing the *causes* of homosexual feelings in men or women, we are most likely observing the *effects* of homosexual behavior upon their physiology.

1 – <u>No one is essentially born with same-sex attraction (SSA)</u>.

There is no compelling scientific evidence that anyone is determined from birth to have SSA. There is no conclusive scientific data that proves there is a simple biological, genetic, or hormonal cause for homosexuality.

2 – <u>No one simply chooses to have SSA</u>.

Same-sex attractions are generally the result of unresolved childhood wounds and unmet needs for love. Homosexual desires arise from a combination of temperamental, environmental, and psychological issues (see the chart Potential Variables Creating Same-Sex Attraction).

3 – <u>People may decide to resolve unwanted SSA</u>.

Research, along with my personal and professional experiences, demonstrates that change is possible. Men and women worldwide have transitioned from a homosexual to heterosexual orientation. Since no one is essentially born with SSA, change is possible.

In our culture and world today, there are many terms loosely used to define someone who experiences SSA: homosexual, bisexual, transgender, gay, and lesbian. Once again, the term "gay" is a socio-political term, which generally applies to an individual who identifies himself or herself as accepting of their SSA, and therefore acts upon those desires. Lesbian refers to a woman who experiences SSA. Bisexual applies to someone who experiences both same and opposite sex attractions. Transgender describes those who believe they were born the wrong sex and wish to live life as the opposite gender. "Non-binary" refers to someone who doesn't identify with either gender, or change their gender identification over time. On Facebook, there are over seventy definitions of gender identity or sexual orientation. The term "sexual orientation" was constructed by members of the gay rights movement. We shall discuss these and other terms in Chapter Four.

There are also those who experience unwanted same-sex attraction and do not identify themselves as "gay," "lesbian," "bisexual," or homosexual. There are young children who experiment with those of the same sex during the onset of adolescence and puberty, as boys are closer to boys at this stage of development, and girls are closer to other girls. This does not make them a person who experiences SSA. There are others who engage in homosexual practices during other stages of their life and move on, for example male students in boarding schools. Likewise, there are men and women who, while incarcerated, engage in homosexual acts but revert to their heterosexuality upon leaving prison. It is only in the last century that we have resorted to labeling people and practices. It is important to remove these labels and understand what drives human behaviors, especially for those who experience same-sex attraction through no fault of their own.

Since the early 1990s, the myth of the "gay gene" and "homosexuality is biological" was promoted throughout the media. A few well-publicized studies launched this campaign to indoctrinate an unsuspecting public into believing that people are born this way and therefore cannot change (as we've seen, these are the two pillars of the homosexual movement). Since then, more studies have appeared trying to prove the "born gay and cannot change" theory. Again, what we are most likely observing are not the causes of SSA, but rather the results of homosexual behavior upon the brain of active SSA men and women.

Dr. Kenneth Klivington, researcher at the Salk Institute in San Diego, CA, stated, "There is a body of evidence that shows the brain's neural networks reconfigure themselves in response to certain experience. Therefore, the difference in homosexual brain structure may be a result of behavior and environmental conditions" (David Gelman et al., "Born or Bred," *Newsweek*, February 24, 1992, p. 46).

Dr. Ruth Hubbard and Dr. Elijah Wald of Harvard University state in their 1993 book, *Exploding the Gene Myth*, "The myth of the all-powerful gene is based on flawed science that discounts the environmental context in which we and our genes exist" (p. 6).

Here are three studies conducted in the 1990s used to advance the homosexual myth in courts and legislative bodies to enact homosexual laws worldwide. With the exception of J. Michael Bailey, these researchers are all gay identified:

Dr. Simon LeVay conducted a study entitled, "A Difference in Hypothalamic Structure between Heterosexual and Homosexual Men," *Science*, August 30, 1991 (Vol. 253, pp. 1034-1037). He observed the brains of men who had died: 19 gay subjects and 16 heterosexual subjects. He professed to have found a group of neurons in the hypothalamus (called INAH3) that appeared to be twice as large in the heterosexual men as in the homosexual men. LeVay theorized that this part of the hypothalamus has something to do with sexual behavior. Therefore, he concluded that sexual orientation is somehow biologically determined. Upon a closer look at his findings, we see many contradictions:

(1) All 19 gay subjects in the study died of AIDS. We know that HIV/AIDS affects the brain causing chemical changes. Therefore, we may be observing the effects of HIV/AIDS on the brain, not the cause of SSA.

(2) Regarding his so-called heterosexual subjects, LeVay states, "Two of these subjects (both AIDS patients) had denied homosexual activity. The records of the remaining

14 patients contained no information about their sexual orientation; they are assumed to have been mostly or all heterosexual" (Ibid, p. 1036). Can you really assume someone is heterosexual because their medical records didn't specify their sexual proclivity? This is hardly science!

In his article, "Salt and Pepper" in the *Bay Area Reporter*, Michael Botkin—homosexual AIDS activist and psychotherapist—stated, "It turns out that LeVay doesn't know anything about the sexual orientation of his control group, the 16 corpses 'presumed heterosexual.' A sloppy control like this is … enough by itself to invalidate the study. LeVay's defense? He knows his controls are het[erosexual] because their brains are different from the HIVer corpses. Sorry, doctor; this is circular logic. You can use the sample to prove the theory or vice versa, but not both at the same time" (September 5, 1991, pp. 21, 24; Source: http://www.leaderu.com/marco/special/spc10.html).

(3) Three of the 19 homosexual subjects had a larger group of neurons in the hypothalamus than the average heterosexual subject. Three of the 16 heterosexual subjects had a smaller group of neurons in the hypothalamus than the average homosexual subject. Six out of 35 subjects disproved LeVay's hypothesis. The results are not statistically significant; they cannot be related to the general population. In order for a study to be seen as valid and reliable, a high enough percentage of subjects must prove the author's theory. This study should never have been published, a fact which many scientists affirmed in the months following its publication.

(4) Finally, LeVay himself stated he did not prove that people are born with SSA: *"It's important to stress what I didn't find. I did not prove that homosexuality is genetic, or find a genetic*

cause for being gay. I didn't show that gay men are born that way, the most common mistake people make in interpreting my work" ("Sex and the Brain," Discover, Vol. 15, no. 3, March 1994, pp. 64-71).

A twin and sibling study was conducted by J. Michael Bailey and Richard Pillard entitled, "A Genetic Study of Male Sexual Orientation." It was published in the *Archives of General Psychiatry*, Vol. 48, December 1991. They observed the prevalence of homosexuality among twins and adopted brothers where at least one brother was same-sex attracted. They found that 52 percent (29 pairs out of 56) of the identical twins were both SSA; 22 percent (12 pairs out of 54) of the fraternal twins were both SSA; and 11 percent (6 of 57) of the adoptive brothers were both SSA. They also found 9 percent (13 of 142) of the non-twin biological siblings were both SSA. The authors then concluded that there must be a genetic basis for SSA. Let us take a closer look and separate fact from fiction:

(1) The biggest flaw is the interpretation of the researchers. Since approximately 50 percent of the identical twins were not SSA, we may easily conclude that genetics does not play a significant role in their homosexuality. If it had, then 100 percent of the twins should be SSA since identical twins have the same genetic makeup. We might just as easily interpret the findings to mean that environmental influences caused their homosexuality. Biology professor and self-proclaimed lesbian Anne Fausto-Stirling of Brown University stated, "In order for such a study to be at all meaningful, you'd have to look at twins raised apart. It's such badly interpreted genetics" (David Gelman et al., "Born or Bred?" *Newsweek*, February 24, 1992, p. 46).

(2) This was not a random sample, but a biased sample, as the twins who volunteered for this study were solicited through

advertisements in LGBTQ+ newspapers and magazines as opposed to general periodicals. If the authors had acquired their subjects from the general population, the percentage of brothers experiencing SSA would have been much smaller. The researchers skewed the data to make it say what they wanted it to say.

Australian researchers observed 33,000 pairs of identical twins from a national database and found that when one twin was SSA, the other twin was SSA only 11% of the time (*Journal of Personality and Social Psychology*, (2000), 78 (3), 524-536).

(3) Dr. LeVay, author of the previous study, stated, "In fact, the twin studies…suggest that it's not totally inborn [homosexuality], because even identical twins are not always of the same sexual orientation" (Quoted in Marlin Maddoux, *Answers to the Gay Deception*, Dallas, TX, International Christian Media, 1994, p. 26).

(4) Dr. Bailey, one of the researchers, stated, "There must be something in the environment to yield the discordant twins" (Gelman, *Newsweek*, 1992, p. 46).

Finally, Dean Hamer and associates from the National Cancer Institute released a study, "A Linkage between DNA Markers on the X Chromosome and Male Sexual Orientation," *Science*, July 16, 1993, Vol. 261, pp. 3212-3217. The media reported immediately that the "gay gene" was discovered. Sorry to disappoint, even Dr. Hammer confessed this was false.

The researchers studied 40 pairs of homosexual brothers and suggested that some cases of homosexuality are linked to a specific region on the X chromosome (Xq28) inherited from the mother by her SSA son(s). Thirty-three pairs of the brothers shared the same pattern variation in the tip of one arm of the chromosome. Hamer estimated that the sequence of the given genetic markers on Xq28 is linked to homosexuality in 64 percent of the brothers. Let's see if his theory holds up under scientific scrutiny:

(1) There was no control group. Hamer and associates failed to test the heterosexual brothers of these SSA men. What if they have the same genetic markers as their SSA brothers?

(2) No one has even proven that the identified section of the chromosome has a direct relationship to sexuality or sexual proclivity.

(3) One of Hamer's research assistants accused him of withholding some of the findings that would have invalidated his study. We have never heard the end result of this investigation by the National Cancer Institute (John Horgan, "Gay Genes, Revisited," *Scientific American*, November, 1995, p. 26).

(4) A group of researchers from the University of Western Ontario under the guidance of Dr. George Rice conducted a study using the same scientific protocol and were unable to produce the same result. ("Where Did the Gay Gene Go?" www.abcnews.com, April 23, 1999).

(5) Hamer himself declared, "These genes do not cause people to become homosexuals…ultimately it is the environment that determines how these genes will express themselves" (*Time*, April 27, 1998, pp. 60-61).

Again, all these researchers, except for J. Michael Bailey, are self-proclaimed gay men. They desperately seek acceptance, and it is their conviction that if we believe they are "born" with SSA, then we must legitimize their homosexual behavior. Instead, we need to reveal the truth behind the homosexual myth, to discover what really causes people to experience same-sex attraction. Here is a more accurate analysis:

> The American College of Pediatricians released a fact sheet about youth in April 2010 stating, "Homosexuality is not a genetically-determined, unchangeable trait. Homosexual attraction is determined by a combination of familial, environmental, social and biological influences. Inheritance of predisposing personality traits may play a role for some. Consequently, homosexual attraction is changeable." (www.FactsAboutYouth.com)

In 2016, Dr. Paul McHugh, former chief psychiatrist at Johns Hopkins University, and Dr. Laurence Mayer, an epidemiologist and professor of psychiatry at Johns Hopkins University, released a report entitled Sexuality and Gender in *The New Atlantis* (www.thenew atlantis.com).

This is a meta-analysis of data from over 200 peer-reviewed studies regarding "sexual orientation" and "gender identity." It is the most objective, exhaustive, and comprehensive study on the topic to date. Highlights of the study:

- "The understanding of sexual orientation as an innate, biologically fixed property of human beings—the idea that people are 'born that way'—is not supported by scientific evidence."
- "Sexual orientation" in adolescents is "fluid over the life course for some people, with one study estimating that as many as 80 percent of male adolescents who report same-sex attractions no longer do so as adults."
- "Compared to heterosexuals, non-heterosexuals are about two to three times as likely to have experienced childhood sexual abuse."

- "Compared to the general population, non-heterosexual sub-populations are at an elevated risk for a variety of adverse health and mental health outcomes."
- "Members of non-heterosexual population are estimated to have about 1.5 times higher risk of experiencing anxiety disorders than members of the heterosexual population, as well as roughly double the risk of depression, 1.5 times the risk of substance abuse, and nearly 2.5 times the risk of suicide."
- "The hypothesis that gender identity is an innate, fixed property of human beings that is independent of biological sex—that a person might be 'a man trapped in a woman's body' or 'a woman trapped in a man's body'—is not supported by scientific evidence."
- "Members of the transgender population are also at higher risk of a variety of mental health problems compared to members of the non-transgender population. Especially alarmingly, the rate of lifetime suicide attempts across all ages of transgender individuals is estimated at 41%, compared to under 5% in the overall U.S. population."
- "Studies comparing the brain structures of transgender and non-transgender individuals … do not provide any evidence for a neurobiological basis for cross-gender identification."
- "Compared to the general population, adults who have undergone sex-reassignment surgery continue to have a higher risk of experiencing poor mental health outcomes. One study found that, compared to controls, sex-reassigned individuals were about five times more likely to attempt suicide and about 19 times more likely to die by suicide."
- "Only a minority of children who experience cross-gender identification will continue to do so into adolescence or adulthood."
- "There is no evidence that all children who express gender-atypical thoughts or behavior should be encouraged to become transgender."

In 2019, a study was published in the journal *Science*, led by a research team from Harvard and MIT, of 470,000 people who identified as gay. They gave permission for their DNA to be tested. This research study was 100 times larger than any group previously studied. They found there was no way to look at someone's DNA and predict whether they were homosexual or heterosexual. Harvard magazine wrote, "There is still no 'gay gene' (https://www.harvard-magazine.com/2019/08/there-s-still-no-gay-gene). Nature magazine reported "No 'gay gene'" (https://www.nature.com/articles/d41586-019-02585-6).

Meaning Behind SSA

Meaning Behind Same-Sex Attraction (SSA)

1. **Homosexuality is a symptom of:**
   - Unhealed wounds of the past (ten potential causes)
   - Unmet needs for love
   - Reparative drive to fulfill homo-emotional and/or homo-social love needs

2. **Homosexuality is essentially an emotionally-based condition:**
   - Need for same-sex parent's / same-sex peers' love
   - Need for gender identification
   - Fear of intimacy with members of the opposite sex

3. **SSA represents a lack of gender identity, caused by either:**
   - Detachment from same-sex parent
   - Detachment from same-sex peers
   - Detachment from one's body
   - Detachment from one's own gender

© Richard Cohen, M.A., 2022

As you will soon discover, there are many contributing factors that lead a boy or girl to develop homosexual feelings. Many professional therapists, myself included, have observed that, most often,

SSA men and women are highly sensitive or hypersensitive individuals. Therefore, they experience life situations and relationships more deeply than other children. This temperament of hypersensitivity often leads these boys and girls to *perceive* rejection from their parents, from their peers, from other family members and friends. This perception becomes their reality: "I don't fit in. I'm different. I don't belong." These are the core beliefs of most children and adolescents who experience SSA.

If you are a parent of a SSA child, please do not blame yourself. This is not a blame game. What I hope to identify here is what may have occurred for the sole purpose of healing and reconciliation. Knowledge is power. Understanding the deeper meaning behind homosexual feelings is instrumental to bring about lasting change.

---

1. Homosexuality is a symptom of:
   - Unhealed wounds of the past (see ten potential causes chart)
   - Unmet needs for love
   - Reparative drive to fulfill homo-emotional and/or homo-social love needs

---

Homosexual feelings, thoughts, and desires are always symptoms of underlying issues. They represent (1) a defensive response to conflicts in the present, a way to medicate pain, (2) unresolved childhood trauma, emotions and wounds that never healed, and (3) a *reparative drive* to fulfill homo-emotional love needs (bonding with same-gender parent, i.e., father-son, mother-daughter) and/or homo-social love needs (bonding with same-gender peers, i.e., guys with guys, girls with girls).

By "reparative drive" we mean that the individual who experiences SSA is seeking to satisfy the love he or she did not attain in early childhood and adolescence, and is doing so by trying to connect with someone of the same sex. This reparative drive is most often completely unconscious. Dr. Elizabeth Moberly coined and Dr. Joseph Nicolosi further developed the concept of homo-emotional love need (read *Homosexuality: A New Christian Ethic* by Moberly and *Reparative Therapy of Male Homosexuality* by Nicolosi).

> 2. Homosexuality is essentially an emotionally based condition:
>   - Need for same-sex parent's / same-sex peers' love
>   - Need for gender identification
>   - Fear of intimacy with members of the opposite sex

We gain our sense of gender identity—masculinity for a man, and femininity for a woman—through successful bonding with our same-sex parent and then same-sex relatives and peers. Most case histories of those who experience SSA demonstrate that homosexual feelings originate in early childhood and preadolescence.

From the ages of one or one-and-a-half to three, the child begins to crawl, walk and then talk. This stage of development is known as a time of separation and individuation. The child begins to realize that she is different from mom, that she is an individual, separate and unique from mother. This time is known as either the terrible or terrific twos, and the operative word is, "No!" "No" essentially means that "I am not you, I am me, and I'm different from you." However, the boy has an extra developmental task here. He comes to realize that his genitals are different from his mother's. Who does he look like, who does he resemble?

The boy must then gender identify with his father, his role model of masculinity. If the father is absent, another male mentor may help stand in the gap for the son. If there is no strong male presence in the toddler's life, he may continue to gender identify with his mother, internalizing her sense of femininity. This is one reason why many men who experience SSA may say, "From the time I was a child, I experienced homosexual feelings." They never successfully individuated from their mothers and gender identified with their fathers. On the other hand, the daughter, even though she is separating and individuating from her mother, will continue to gender identify with mom as her primary role model of femininity. She individuates while continuing to emulate her mother's behaviors. In the case of a potential SSA daughter, she may have been fearful of or repelled by her mother, and therefore didn't successfully internalize her own sense of femaleness (see other causes listed below).

Same-sex attraction often represents a search for parenting—a man seeking paternal love in the arms of another man, and a woman seeking maternal love in the arms of another woman (of course, this drive may be completely unconscious). It may also represent a need for bonding with same-sex peers because these men and women never experienced successful bonding with those of the same sex in their preadolescent and/or adolescent years of development. Then, during puberty, those normal needs for bonding, with same-sex parent and/or same-sex peers, became sexualized and/or eroticized. At this point the world says to such a person, "You're born gay," or "You're born lesbian." This is a false label.

Labeling people with words like gay, lesbian, bisexual, or transgender is not only false, it also is done without a proper understanding of the situation. We are born as a man or a woman, as a son or a daughter. Those who experience SSA are merely stuck in early stages of psychosexual development. When they resolve past issues and fulfill unmet love needs in healthy, nonsexual, same-sex relationships, they will naturally develop opposite-sex desires. We are all heterosexually designed (men and women fit together beautifully and perfectly, biologically two men or two women simply do not).

If a man seeks to join sexually with another man, it means there is something lacking within him. He does not experience the fullness of his own masculinity. By joining with a man, he hopes to complete this lost part of himself. The same holds true for the woman seeking to join sexually with another woman. These yearnings represent the deep need of a child within—a need to experience love and secure bonding with someone of the same sex, to restore this lack of love. However, sexual relations will never satiate that need for love because it is that of a child, and children do not want or need sex.

In many cases men who experience SSA have been over-attached to their mothers and detached from their fathers and the masculinity they represented. As a result of closeness to his mom and detachment from his dad, the son becomes internally more feminine in nature. In adulthood, this may block his ability to have a successful heterosexual relationship with another woman, because of this over-attachment and identification with the feminine (remember, opposites attract). The same may hold true for the daughter who is over attached to her father and disconnected and dis-identified with her mother. She internalizes her dad's masculinity and rejects her mother's femininity. She may spend the rest of her life looking for that lost love and sense of connection with the feminine in the arms of other women.

Many women who experience SSA have been detached from their mothers. They might have also been sexually, physically, emotionally, and/or mentally abused by men, rejected by female peers, and/or are highly sensitive. Not wanting to re-experience abuse with men, many turn to other women for affection, comfort and love. It is interesting to note that there is a higher percentage of domestic violence among lesbian couples than there is in the heterosexual population. Why? Underneath the exterior of these women are hurt little girls who were violated, who take out their aggression and unresolved pain on each other.

The father of Sarah, a SSA woman, had had many affairs. He was loud, angry, judgmental, and strict. Sarah developed anxiety around her dad as well as other men, and therefore turned to women for her affectional needs, seeking safety in their arms. Another SSA woman, Crystal, had parents who were always busy. She felt invisible to them.

She clung to her brothers for attention and affection, even though they mistreated and abused her. Crystal feared revealing her heart to anyone, and longs for a woman to just hold her in her arms. You will also learn about another woman who experienced SSA, Susan, whose story appears after Chapter Three.

Psychotherapist Janelle Hallman, in her landmark book, *The Heart of Female Same-Sex Attraction* (InterVarsity Press, 2008), mentions four types of profiles about women who experience SSA. "They are primarily descriptive in nature and should *not* be rigidly construed: indeed, many women *may* identify with one profile over another, but will most likely see parts of themselves in each of the other profiles as well" (p. 159).

"Profile 1: Empty, Depressed, Withdrawn and Isolated. These women often have profound developmental deficits arising out of perceived and actual emotional absence or neglect. Their basic physical needs were met, but they nevertheless internalized the message that their existence was an inconvenience and a nuisance. Their lives are severely empty and lonely. They have a few friends, but the friendships lack mutuality. They feel more attached to objects or animals than to people. They are uncomfortable in their own skin and know that they are not 'normal,' at least in social settings. They may show marked inability to follow standard social cueing or comprehend— let alone articulate—inner emotional or psychological dynamics. They are often overweight and tend to be nondescript in appearance" (p. 160).

"Profile 2: Tough, Angry, Sarcastic and Barricaded. These women often have the worst histories of trauma and abuse, frequently involving severe physical or emotional abandonment, although this is not always the case. For some, the environments in which they were raised were not hostile, but the women nevertheless sensed and were negatively affected by the underlying relational dysfunctions within the family system. Both groups of women carry a deep belief that the world is not safe. They have relied on toughness (rather than the deadness found among profile 1 women) to protect their tender hearts. They are often overwhelmingly disillusioned to discover that their method of survival—severe defensiveness—actually starves them of intimacy. Unlike those associated with profile 1, they can feel their inner agony and therefore aggressively and continuously 'cut off' all vulnerabilities. They work hard but are demanding; they are impatient but also deeply committed. If they decide that you are safe, they will do anything in the world for you. They have an endless ability to care for and take care of others, all the while denying their own needs" (p. 165).

"Profile 3: Energetic, Caretaking, Drama-Oriented, and never 'Home.' Even though these women are less likely to have typical trauma or neglect in their background as compared to women associated with profiles 1 and 2, they still suffer from severe, subtle and negative relational dynamics such as familial enmeshment or rigid gender roles within their families of origin. Due to their attuned sensitivities and perhaps their deeper relational needs, they felt that they were neither acknowledged nor affirmed as special, particularly as a girl. Although they felt close and loved, they also felt obligated to support or take care of other family members, including Mom and Dad. Nevertheless, their basic needs were usually met, and they experience the greatest level of stability among the four profiles. They are active, often athletic and typically overachieving women" (p. 170).

"Profile 4: Pragmatic, Perfectionistic, Distant and Smugly Self-Assured. Women with this profile have various backgrounds but typically compensate for their losses and defend against their pain by avoiding all vulnerability and identifying with their ability to pursue excellence and success. They are often the movers and shakers within their field of expertise and find their kudos through achievement. They are very intelligent and extremely gifted. But because they are often so accomplished, they are also arrogant and contemptuous of others (especially men). They may unconsciously use others to serve their own purpose or meet their own needs" (p. 176).

Dr. Hallman concludes by appealing to her reader: *Please do not reduce a SSA woman to one profile. There is more to her than a simple description. The only useful purpose of these categories is to learn how to assist each woman in her healing process.* I hope you'll read Janelle's book for a more comprehensive understanding of female SSA.

---

3. SSA represents a lack of gender identity, caused by either:
   - Detachment from same-sex parent
   - Detachment from same-sex peers
   - Detachment from one's body
   - Detachment from one's own gender

Same-sex attractions may represent detachment between the individual and his or her same-sex parent and/or same-sex peers. Because the boy did not successfully or sufficiently bond with his dad and/or other male peers, he then rejects his own gender identity, not wanting to act or be like his father or other boys. After this occurs and puberty sets in, his emotional needs for bonding become sexualized. This is the construction of SSA and perhaps a gay identity—little boys and girls in adolescent or adult bodies looking for bonding through sexual relationships. Sexual behavior cannot and will not resolve their deeper needs.

Ten Potential Causes of SSA

I came out of homosexuality myself. I understand this condition from the inside out. I have been married over 42 years. Many reporters have asked me, "Would you love your son or daughter if they were homosexual?" My answer is always the same, "Of course I would, but that would never happen because I know what causes someone to experience same-sex attraction." And yes, all three of my kids are heterosexual. Our sons are manly and also sensitive. Our daughter is both feminine and powerful.

As a psychotherapist, I have helped hundreds of men and women who experienced unwanted SSA achieve their heterosexual potential and dreams. There is no such thing as a homosexual (noun). There are only people who experience same-sex attraction (adjective) and practice homosexual behaviors—for many different reasons.

The following is a list of ten potential causes that may lead an individual to experience SSA (see the chart at the beginning of this chapter). A combination of experiences and characteristics lead to SSA—never a single factor alone. Parents do not instill SSA in their children. It is the child's perception of their parenting combined with his/her innate temperament, e.g. hypersensitivity, which makes the difference. To see how these factors interact and create SSA in children, please read the case histories of the five celebrities in the next chapter. You may also want to watch wonderful stories of transformation at http://www.voicesofchange.net.

1. Heredity

- Unresolved family issues
- Misperceptions
- Tendency to feel rejected

"It is assumed [by intergenerational and transgenerational family systems theory] that relational patterns are learned and passed down across the generations and that current individual and family behavior is a result of these patterns" ("Assessment of Intergenerational Family Relationships," *Family of Origin Therapy*, James Bray and Donald Williamson, Rockville, MD, Aspen Publishers, 1987, p. 31).

In family systems therapy, it is well known and accepted that unresolved issues and dysfunctional behaviors of preceding generations are passed down to subsequent family members. At the core of an individual who experiences SSA is a sense of not belonging, not fitting in, and feeling different from others. These thoughts and feelings may be inherited from family members depending upon their circumstances in life, culture, religion, race, and/or ethnicity.

What I and other sexual orientation therapists have observed is that men and women who experience SSA are highly susceptible to rejection, or perceived rejection, existing for any number of reasons which may stem from unresolved generational issues. Of course, this does not cause same-sex attraction in boys or girls; it is just one contributing factor among many.

2. Temperament

- Hypersensitive
- Artistic nature
- Gender nonconforming behaviors:
  Male more feminine; female more masculine

As I have mentioned, many or most SSA men and women as children were highly sensitive, or hypersensitive, which led them to react more deeply to the behaviors of their parents, relatives and peers. Often attuned to the emotions of their parents, these children will frequently modify their behaviors to avoid conflict. Other times, they will become pleasers or caretakers. Because of their hypersensitive nature, they may act more passively and therefore be unable to assert themselves in interpersonal relationships. Of course, not all sensitive children will develop SSA.

If the hypersensitive child has an artistic nature, and the parents, relatives or peers are non-supportive of this gift, she or he may experience further rejection. The sensitive and gifted child, in an insensitive and non-support environment, experiences undue stress and anxiety.

A further group of young children, who exhibit what we call "gender non-conforming behaviors," that is, the little boy who acts more effeminate and the little girl who acts more masculine, are particularly at risk for being either ostracized by family members and peers, or these days, encouraged to act upon those tendencies (the new transgender phenomenon). However, these character traits—(or behavioral phenotypes), the more effeminate boy and more masculine girl—in certain environments are expressed with the purpose of invoking a reparative or healing drive. By that I mean that a child is seeking to successfully bond with his or her same-sex parent, and thus not trying to summon a gay identity. When this drive for bonding is achieved, the child will have a healthy attachment with his or her same-sex parent and secure gender identity will ensue.

Therefore, with this understanding, instead of thinking, "Oh, he was born gay," or "She was meant to be a boy," and with deeper insight into the dynamics of the family system, we see an attempt by the birth of this child to heal generational wounds of detachment between either fathers and sons or mothers and daughters. If the father would take the time to join with this effeminate boy, see life through his eyes and experiences, eventually the boy will bond with his dad and internalize his father's sense of masculine identity. The same would hold true for the mother and her more masculine daughter.

Dr. Francis S. Collins, director of the National Institutes for Health and former director of the Human Genome Project, declares that homosexuality is "genetically influenced but not hardwired by DNA, and that whatever genes are involved represent predispositions, not predeterminations" (*The Language of God*, New York, 2006, Free Press, p. 260). With healthy intervention and parenting/mentoring, the child will experience a sense of his or her own gender identity and opposite-sex desires with ensue.

3. Opposite-Gender (Hetero-Emotional) Parental Wounds

- Over attachment to opposite-sex parent (enmeshment)
- Imitation of opposite-sex behaviors
- Abuse: emotional, mental, verbal, physical, and/or sexual

There has been much literature written about boys over-attached to their mothers and girls over-attached to their fathers. Again, this is not a blame game, but naming what took place for the purpose of healing. Drs. Irving Bieber, Charles Socarides, Joseph Nicolosi,

Gerard van den Aardweg, Sigmund Freud, Robert Kronemeyer and many other psychologists and psychiatrists have observed that men who experience SSA have had an abnormally close mother-son attachment. They are inclined to internalize their mother's sense of femininity and become distant and detached from the masculinity represented by their fathers. On the other hand, the daughter may be closer to her father and estranged from her mother, thereby internalizing her father's masculinity and rejecting her mother's femininity. In other cases, the daughter views the mother as weak and/or ineffective, and models her behavior after the more dominant and powerful parent, her father.

Another phenomenon might be the child perceiving that his or her parents wanted a child of the opposite sex. The son therefore acts like a girl, and the daughter acts like a boy in order to please their parents and win their approval and affection.

As mentioned, many women who experience SSA have been abused by men, and not wanting to repeat these unhealthy bonding patterns, they seek their affectional needs from women.

4. Same-Gender (Homo-Emotional) Parental Wound

- Detachment from same-sex parent
- Neglect: lack of intimacy
- Abuse: emotional, mental, verbal, physical, and/or sexual

Lack of sufficient bonding between the son and his father and daughter and her mother is often at the core of anyone who experiences SSA (homo-emotional wound). Some of the experiences of detachment/neglect may be an angry, violent or scary parent, a physically or emotionally unavailable parent, etc., Additionally, because of the hypersensitive temperament, it may be the perception of the child who feels rejected and detaches. For whatever reason(s), many children who experience SSA did not securely connect with the same-sex parent. The mismatch in character and temperament between father and son or mother and daughter often creates the sense of hurt in the heart of a pre-SSA child. Without the parent perceiving these cues, the daughter or son becomes susceptible to further rejection by same-sex peers. The stage is then set for the potential development of same-sex attraction and same-sex erotic feelings during or after puberty. Those desires represent a means to achieve bonding that never took place in the earliest years of child development.

5. Sibling Wounds / Family Dynamics

- Name calling
- Same-sex siblings/relative's rejection
- Abuse: emotional, mental, verbal, sexual, and/or physical

Yet another variable that may contribute to the development of SSA is insufficient bonding with siblings and/or relatives of the same sex, e.g., boys with brothers and male relatives, or girls with sisters and female relatives. These sensitive children are often people-pleasers, trying to keep everyone happy at the expense of their own needs. Over the past 35 years as a psychotherapist, I have heard so many parents say, "My son was the perfect little boy." Well, boys generally by nature are more assertive and mischievous, and not so sweet. Be careful of the "good little boys," encourage them to be themselves and not to please everyone else.

Some women who experience SSA had poor relationships with their sisters, and/ or were mocked and teased by men in their family. This leaves a deep wound in their hearts, not fitting in with their same-sex peers and relatives, and feeling hurt by men. Some boys who experience SSA grew up in families of all girls and women, and some SSA girls grew up in families of all men. These factors may also contribute to gender confusion.

6. Body Image Wounds

- Late bloomer
- Shorter/taller—thinner/larger
- Physical disability

Late bloomer, early maturation, physical disabilities, shorter, taller, thinner, or larger—these are some characteristics that may result in body-image wounds for the pre-SSA boy or girl. A hypersensitive boy who experienced insufficient bonding with his father and over-attachment with his mother, now incurs more self-esteem issues by being different from other guys, e.g., too tall, too thin, too short, too large, not athletically inclined. The result is a profound sense of gender inadequacy, feeling on the outside looking in. If they were late bloomers, they often felt different and alienated from their peers. And the pre-SSA girl may experience similar thoughts and feelings based upon her perception of her body image and the opinions of her parents, relatives and/or peers.

7. Sexual Abuse

- Homosexual imprinting
- Learned and reinforced behaviors
- Substitute for affection and love

Sexual abuse may be another contributing factor to the development of same-sex attraction, however, it is never the sole cause. The pre-SSA child is more susceptible to sexual abuse because of his or her lack of attachment to same-sex parent and/or same-sex peers. Sex then becomes a substitute or replacement for emotional and relational intimacy with others of the same sex. If the behavior is repeated over time, it may create a neurological basis for the further development of same-sex attraction in the male or female. Again, this is just another contributing factor and not a prerequisite to experience SSA. In my therapy practice, and the counseling practice of many colleagues, approximately 50% of our clients experienced some form of childhood sexual abuse.

There is usually a difference between SSA men and women when it comes to sexual abuse. Many boys who carry father and/or male peer wounds were easy targets for male sexual abuse, because they were longing for that connection with their dads and other guys. Many girls who develop SSA were sexually abused by men. They may seek female affection to soothe their wounds and protect themselves from further abuse by men.

8. Same-Sex (Homo-Social) Peer Wounds

- Name calling / put-downs
- Teacher's pet
- Non-athletic boy / more athletic girl

Both men and women who experience SSA often felt a tremendous sense of emotional wounding because of same-sex peer rejection—guys didn't fit in with other guys, and girls didn't fit in with other girls. Often they were called names such as "sissy," "faggot," "queer," "pansy," "dyke," "tomboy." Many boys who experience SSA hung out with the girls, and girls who experience SSA hung out with the guys. While boys who experience SSA were not athletically inclined and received teasing and taunting from their male peers, some girls who experience SSA were more athletic, and if detached from their female peers, may have been ostracized as well. Then, during or after adolescence, those normal needs for same-sex peer bonding became sexualized.

Another source of wounding for the pre-SSA child is boys mocking girls ("You're so butch," "You're a dyke") and girls mocking boys ("You're such a faggot," "You're so sweet and girlie"). Not only do they receive put-downs from their same-sex peers, but opposite sex peers as well.

9. Cultural Wounds

- Promotion of the homosexual myth—born that way and cannot change
- Cultural Abuse: media, Internet, educational system, and politics affirm and promote homosexuality
- Pornography

After a boy or girl experiences wounding or lack of attachment with their same-sex parent and/or peers, or incurs any of the other factors previously mentioned, then same-sex attractions develop during or after adolescence leading to homo-erotic feelings and desires. The world then mistakenly says, "You're gay," or "You're lesbian." As we have learned, this is a false paradigm leading hurt children down the road to homosexuality under false pretenses. Also, with behaviors from performers in the music and entertainment industries, it is becoming trendy to experiment sexually and identify as LGBTQ+, non-binary, etc.

Many kids are being raised in single-parent families, often lacking the attention and affection of the same-sex parent. This leaves him or her vulnerable to being enrolled into the false gay paradigm, whereby their normal needs for bonding will become eroticized by members of the same sex. The media, educational system and the entertainment industry, driven by the homosexual myth, have created false identities: LGBTQ+. But there is no such thing as a "gay." There are only hurt children looking for love in ways that will not fulfill their deepest desires for real love.

Again we go back to the Homosexual Manifesto and the false indoctrination of our youth and our culture into the innate, immutable paradigm. If boys or girls experience SSA in adolescence, we immediately label them as gay, rather than understand there are specific causes that led him or her to experience SSA. No one is born this way. There are always reasons why anyone develops homosexual feelings. (Remember, some kids experiment with same-sex friends at the onset of adolescence, but this does not make them gay or SSA.)

10. Other Factors

- Divorce
- Death
- Adoption
- Religion
- Spiritual factors

There are any number of other life experiences that may contribute towards the development of SSA and low self-worth in a sensitive boy or girl. If the parents divorce, the people-pleasing child may blame himself or herself. If a parent dies, the child may perceive it as personal rejection and abandonment. When a struggling child hears "hell and damnation" or homosexuality is an "abomination" from the pulpit of his or her place of worship, further feelings of guilt and shame burden this sensitive child (read the story of Kevin Jennings in the next chapter).

If the child was adopted, she or he may feel rejected by their birth parents and never securely attach to their adopted parents (read Greg Louganis's story in the next chapter). This sense of rejection may reside deep in the unconscious, creating a pattern of insecurity.

Note: Many people with a strong faith background believe there might be spiritual influences that drive homosexual feelings in boys or girls and men or women. Even if there is validity to this, it is imperative to realize that when the other ten potential factors are addressed, healing occurs and change will ensue. By strictly viewing SSA as a "spiritual problem," one will not fully heal and fulfill their innate heterosexual potential. As psychotherapist Jan Frank stated, "You cannot heal a spirit, or deliver a wound."

"For a homosexual adaptation to occur, in our time and culture, these factors must combine to (1) create an impaired gender-identity [feeling of masculinity or femininity], (2) create a fear of intimate contact with members of the opposite sex, and (3) provide opportunities for sexual release with members of the same sex" (Dr. Judd Marmor, as quoted in *Growing Up Straight*, Peter and Barbara Wyden, New York: Stein and Day, 1968, p. 18).

A combination of any of these ten factors may lead an individual to experience SSA: (1) Heredity, (2) Temperament, (3) Hetero-emotional wounds, (4) Homo-emotional wounds, (5) Sibling wounds and family dynamics, (6) Body-image wounds, (7) Sexual abuse, (8) Social and peer wounds, (9) Cultural wounds, and (10) Other factors. *The severity of wounding in each category will have a direct impact upon the amount of time and effort it will take to heal.*

Please read my book *Being Gay: Nature, Nurture or Both?* for a greater explanation about the potential causes of SSA, and a four-stage model of healing, plus remarkable stories of change.

> *- No one is essentially born with SSA.*
> *- No one chooses to have SSA.*
> *- The only choice is to live a homosexual life*
> *or resolve unwanted SSA.*

Let me make it perfectly clear: I am not saying that people who decide to live a homosexual life are wrong. I respect all members of the LGBTQ+ community and the path that they have chosen. For me, I chose a different path, the road less traveled, and, as Robert Frost has written, that has made all the difference. What I wish to convey is that people are not essentially born with SSA, and that change is possible for those who pursue this option. The fact that there are underlying causes of homosexual feelings and there exists the potential for change is *not* widely publicized. There has existed for decades a heavily financed media mechanism, which would have us believe the opposite.

Seven Stages of "Coming Out"

To better understand the heart and mind of those who experience SSA, I would now like to share with you the seven stages leading to the "coming out" process. The following descriptions come from my book *Gay Children, Straight Parents* (pp. 18-22):

Stage 1 – Causes of SSA

Stage 2 – Same-sex attractions begin

Stage 3 – Conflict over SSA

Stage 4 – Need for belonging

Stage 5 – Indoctrination

Stage 6 – Identity acceptance as gay, lesbian, bisexual, transgender, non-binary

Stage 7 – "Coming out" process

Stage 1: Causes of SSA. We just mentioned the many contributing factors that result in homosexual desires such as disrupted attachment between father and son or mother and daughter (this may be the child's perception, not the parent's failure), over-attachment to the opposite-sex parent, hypersensitivity, lack of bonding with same-gender peers, sibling wounds, cultural wounds, name-calling, sexual abuse and body image wounds. Again, it is never one thing alone that causes SSA but a combination of factors.

Stage 2: Same-sex attractions begin. SSA begins at various ages for different people depending on several factors: the child's temperament, physiology and perceptions; family history at particular times; and social or cultural events. Most often, the eroticization of another person of the same sex begins around ten to thirteen years of age, near the onset of puberty. In some cases the desires may occur sooner, if a child has undergone sexual abuse or some other signifi-cant trauma (e.g. early exposure to sexuality). For others, homosexual desires may emerge later on, in the late teens or early twenties, or in some cases during a mid-life crisis. More and more married men and women are "coming out" and often times disclosing their long battle with SSA. Such people repressed their same-sex attractions for many years, hoping and praying they would disappear.

Stage 3: Conflict over SSA. The young struggler may ask him-self, "Why do I have these feelings? What would others think of me if they knew I had homosexual desires?" A child may wonder, "Is it a sin to feel this way? Does God still love me?" Most often, these boys and girls experience tremendous feelings of pain, confusion, guilt, shame, and loneliness. These emotions are exacerbated when the young person is unable or unwilling to talk freely with family and friends. Other times, she or he may be involved in a strong religious community, and to disclose about her or his SSA is too scary for fear of being judged and rejected.

Kids today easily find "answers" outside their immediate circle of loved ones and spiritual community. They access pro-homosexual information on the Internet or attend a Gay Straight Alliance (GSA) meeting in middle and high school, or a LGBTQ+ club in college. The new addition to the LGBTQ+ nomenclature is "Q" meaning "Queer" or "Questioning" youth, so that people who have a fleeting attraction for someone of the same sex may be led to believe that they are gay, bisexual or queer.

As mentioned, some young children experiment with members of their own sex while entering into adolescence. Others have had sexual encounters while intoxicated, and others while attending boarding school. This does not make these young people same-sex attracted or gay. This is situational behavior and the majority of these people move on to develop strictly heterosexual feelings and desires.

Stage 4: Need for belonging. The struggle continues: "I don't fit in. I don't belong. I'm not like the other kids." During puberty, what were once emotional desires for bonding with same-sex parent and/or same-sex peers, now become sexually inflamed yearnings. The emotional need for nonsexual intimacy with the same-sex parent and/or same-sex peers suddenly becomes eroticized. However intense the desire may feel, it is important to remember that the basis for all SSA is unmet love needs and lack of sufficient gender identity, not sexual attraction.

Stage 5: Indoctrination. As we see in the world today, any young person who experiences the least amount of same-sex attraction is told, "You were born gay. You cannot change. Efforts to change are harmful." These youngsters have to work very hard to accept themselves as gay, lesbian, bisexual or queer. This process generates conflicting thoughts and feelings. I believe that those who experience SSA initially know, in their conscience, that homosexual behavior is out of sync with natural law. Nonetheless, they are inundated with the idea that SSA is genetically, biologically or hormonally determined—they're born that way, therefore, they cannot change.

The "born gay" myth is much like the old folk tale *The Emperor's New Clothes*. In this story, an emperor is fooled into believing skilled craftsmen are creating beautiful clothes for him. In fact, two charlatans create nothing. Going along with the hoax, the emperor parades through the city streets wearing nothing but his underwear. Not wanting to appear foolish, all his subjects exclaim, "What a wonderful set of new clothes!" Then a child stands up and says, "The emperor is naked!" At that moment the emperor realizes he has been duped. "We should all be like this child and speak the truth," he proclaims.

So it is today. Most of us have been deceived, even though we instinctively know that humans are heterosexually designed: a man and a woman fit perfectly together and two men or two women do not.

Stage 6: Identity acceptance as gay, lesbian, bisexual,, transgender or queer. At this juncture, strugglers come to terms with their SSA and adopt a gay, lesbian, bisexual, transgender, queer, or non-binary identity. They have anesthetized their conscience through social indoctrination and finally self-acceptance. Hearing the homosexual myth repeated often enough, with little or no debate, establishes it as "fact." At this stage, you and the rest of the "homophobic" society may be perceived as the enemy. (A phobia is an irrational fear of something, not a principled disagreement. Gay activists have mis-used this term.) "You don't understand. You don't know what it's like to be gay and be on the outside looking in." The us-versus-them mentality is reinforced.

Stage 7: "Coming out" process. Often parents are the last to know about a child's SSA, not because they are the least important, but because they are the most important. Gender-confused young people are especially sensitive and fearful of rejection, so they first "come out" to their friends, teachers or relatives who seem to be safer. They are developing a support system fearing that mom and/or dad may reject them. Finally, he may share with his parents, "Please accept me for who I am. I'm your gay child. God made me this way!" Or she may angrily exclaim, "If you refuse to accept me just the way I am, you're homophobic and unloving." The truth is, they are afraid to lose their parents' love.

What if you find it difficult to accept a family member or friend's homosexual identity and/or lifestyle? How do you love them without endorsing something you may not believe in? This will be the subject in Chapter Five. The path of "coming out" is most often lonely and painful, frequently walked alone. Today, strugglers get support from LGBTQ+ groups on-line or at their local Gay Straight Alliance in school. The sad thing is that young people are totally unaware that there are alternatives to living a homosexual life.

Resolving Unwanted SSA *Is* Possible

> Dr. Robert Spitzer, former professor of psychiatry at Columbia University, stated, "Like most psychiatrists, I thought that homosexual behavior could only be resisted, and that no one could really change their sexual orientation. I now believe that to be false. *Some people can and do change*" (*Archives of Sexual Behavior*, October 2003, Vol. 32, No. 5, pp. 403-417).

Over the past thirty-five years as a psychotherapist, I have had the privilege of assisting those who experience unwanted SSA achieve their heterosexual dreams. I know personally and professionally that *Change Is Possible!* My life is a testament to this fact, as are the lives of thousands of other men and women worldwide who have come out of homosexuality. Since people are not essentially born with SSA, the opportunity for transformation is available for those who seek change.

Keys to healing unwanted same-sex attraction are: (1) discovering the root causes of SSA—the hidden meaning behind the desires, (2) healing wounds of the past—one must feel in order to heal, (3) gaining support from others—SSA men healing with OSA (Opposite-Sex Attracted) men and SSA women with OSA women, and (4) experiencing the love of God. Personal motivation is imperative if someone wants to change. In Chapter Five, I will share practical suggestions how to help those who are gay identified fulfill their true gender identity.

It is also important for someone seeking to come out of SSA to find effective counseling. I mention "effective" counseling because most therapists do not have a clue how to assist those who experience unwanted SSA. Since 1973, there has been little or no training of therapists in this field of sexual orientation therapy (view our Counselor Training Program film series and manual: https://www.pathinfo. org/counselor-training-program-film-ser). Dr. Joseph Nicolosi, Sr.

coined the term Reparative Therapy which has been pejoratively labeled "Conversion Therapy." The Alliance for Therapeutic Choice and Scientific Integrity is dedicated to assisting those who experience unwanted SSA (https://www.therapeuticchoice.com). Members are therapists, educators, and concerned citizens. You may contact them for a referral therapist in your area or country. Be aware that some of those therapists may be sympathetic to this issue; however, they may not have specific training in this field. Please see the Resource section at the end of this book for a list of therapeutic organizations and ministries assisting those who experience unwanted SSA and their loved ones.

Interview candidates if you seek a therapist. You may ask them the following questions: (1) what is your education and training in the field of sexual orientation therapy, reparative therapy, or gender-affirming therapy?; (2) How long have you worked in this field and what is your success rate?; (3) What therapeutic approaches do you use in helping people resolve their unwanted SSA? (Please read Chapters Four and Six in my book *Being Gay: Nature, Nurture or Both?* to better understand the healing process and therapeutic modalities); (4) Do you really believe that people can change?; and (5) Do you believe in God (if this is important to you)? The individual seeking help is going to be sharing very deeply and entrusting the therapist with guiding him or her on this journey of healing. It is essential that you understand the therapist's education, training, success rate, therapeutic approaches, and perspective on this controversial issue. Set up a free 15-20 minute in-person, telephone, or on-line consultation before making a commitment to enter therapy.

Marriage is *never* the solution for SSA. Why? Because a woman can never meet the homo-emotional/homo-social love needs of a man, and a man can never meet the homo-emotional/homo-social love needs of a woman. In the process of healing, first a man who experiences SSA must heal with OSA men, and a woman who experiences SSA must heal with OSA women. I was told, "Find the right woman and she'll straighten you out." Well, I did, and she didn't. Not because she couldn't, but because there were so many wounds in my heart that needed to be healed. Like every other man who experiences unwanted SSA, I needed to first securely bond with healthy, heterosexual men in order to experience my own manliness before being successful as a husband and father. I made all the mistakes possible, thereby becoming an excellent therapist and coach for those seeking change! And I'm not the only one. Thousands of men and women worldwide have changed and fulfilled their heterosexual potential. As Winston Churchill declared, *"Never give up!"* SSA is a message from the soul trying to teach the individual about himself or herself.

With these principles in mind, I hope you'll enjoy reading the story of Christian.

Christian's Story

It was July 1995 and I had come to the end of a very long, long road. I was gay—a homosexual. It was a time to give up the charade I had been playing for forty-four years. It was a deep, dark secret I had hidden from everyone. This feeling of gayness had been a part of every aspect of my life, and I could no longer tolerate the incredible pain. I supposedly had it all. I had a great job and social life. I had the suburban lifestyle. I had a beautiful, devoted, loving wife of over twenty years and the greatest daughter and son a father could ever hope for. Ultimately, however, I always felt trapped as a homosexual pretending to be a straight man in a straight world where I just didn't belong. It was time to come out as a gay man.

I grew up as a kid in the 1950s and went to college in the late '60s. I was not part of the pre-"coming out" acceptance of gays in the 1970s. As a child, teenager, and college student, there was no one available in the public sector to openly go to for support. "Queers" and "fags" was the terminology I knew, and I certainly felt that I fit the mold. It was always too frightening as a kid and young adult to actually admit I was queer. I thought if I just play the part of a straight man, maybe it will all go away. The general public did not accept gayness; it was definitely taboo.

With the 1970s a flood of information came to me from strong, openly gay men and women. The media blitz and the changing world were letting me know that, "Hey, you're gay, and it's okay." It was not okay with me. I had already married and started a family. I ached to be a part of the gay scene, but I also ached for my sexual feelings to just go away. I was upset with and jealous of gay men because I felt alone, isolated, and detached from any identification with heterosexual or homosexual men.

Up to the early 1980s, I had only once gone to a Christian counselor about my "depression." He informed me I was a latent homosexual, probably should break off my engagement and look at nude pictures of women to get the "cure." Needless to say, I dismissed his advice and pretended this counseling had never occurred.

By the early1980s, I was like a volcano ready to explode. I had never had a sexual encounter with a man. I had lots of fantasies and wet dreams, but never actual physical encounters. Theater had been a way for me to be around and near gay men. It was after a theatrical performance I confessed to a friend, who was gay, that I had sexual feelings for men. Soon after this confession, I got invited to his apartment where he introduced me to homosexual sex. It was like thirty years of dead, suppressed weight lifted from me. I soon found another cast member who was more than willing to engage in sex with the new gay on the block. I thought I was in heaven, but it quickly turned into hell. I felt empty, alone, frightened, deceitful, guilty, dirty, and ultimately, heading in a direction where I did not want to go.

I was living a double life. I confessed to my wife that I was gay. She did not accept this as truth. She knew I was not gay, but her ability to help me was just not there. A straight psychologist tried to help me, but he had no clue what to do. He knew I wanted to stay married, but did not know how to help me. I read some literature and got the idea that this was genetic and that was that. To help support the genetic theory, my sister had just confessed to the family that she was gay! I dropped the psychologist, and my wife and I pretended that the problem went away. I hated myself.

A few years after this, in the mid 1980s, I had again stayed away from gay sexual encounters. However, my wife's and my sexual life was in shambles. I hated sex with my wife. This was not the best criterion for wedded bliss. She sent me off to a New Age encounter with some guru who could "zap" the homosexuality out of me. I was desperate and scared, so I agreed to go. It was horrific. I question if this man was possessed by some demon that really wanted to suck out my soul. He worked by intimidating and humiliating me in front of hundreds of his followers. He pronounced that I was the devil and for his followers to shun and stay away from me. I fled this scene and was sure any hope of ridding myself of gayness was totally unrealistic. I again began to periodically engage in sexual encounters with men. It became both an addiction and a short-lived fix. I could go months without having sex with a man, but then if something happened in my life that was stressful, I would flee for a homosexual encounter. I kept searching for the perfect man, and I somehow believed that if I found him, he would be strong enough and love me enough to take me away from the straight world. I would then be safe, warm, and loved. As the years passed, I realized that this was a fantasy that just wasn't coming true.

So, I take you back to July 1995. My anxiety level was about to explode. With deep regret, I had secretly begun to see a counselor to help me transition out of my heterosexual marriage to the gay community. I felt thoroughly depressed, but felt I had *no other choice* for the sake of my wife and for my survival. At the same time, my wife presented me with a book written by Richard Cohen. She had seen Richard on a TV show many months before. She had diligently tracked down this book. On this TV show, Richard claimed he could transition men from homosexuality to heterosexuality. I was furious and skeptical. I decided no more wacko gurus for me. It was garbage. My wife then gave me the best ultimatum of my life: "Go see Richard, or move out and get a divorce." I loved her enough to try one more time, but felt it was another hopeless course.

I was totally and utterly skeptical of therapy that gave me a choice to be straight. I was too old at forty-four to change. There could be no magical "hocus-pocus." I had my feet firmly planted in the genetic theory. My childhood encounters and my parents had nothing to do with this gayness that I felt. Richard Cohen's therapy *would not work*.

I wish there were a way to convey true gut feelings. It was a dark, broken individual who had his first therapy session with Richard. For me, building a trusting relationship with him was the key that began to open the door of healing for me. Being able to pour out my true feelings to someone who was really listening was an important first step. He had walked the walk, so I could accept what was truth for him. His living example gave me the initial prospect that healing just might be possible. I knew I wanted to transition, so I would take it one day at a time.

I began to learn that there were major key factors that contributed to my homo-emotional feelings. It was important for me to learn that my same-sex attractions were the sum of many key factors. My childhood, in my eyes, had been perfect. My parents had provided me with a beautiful home, clothes, food, and social and travel experiences. An incredible realization was that neither of my parents was demonstrative in physical touch or verbal affirmations. I have no memory of either of my parents ever telling me they loved me. I have only one memory of my mom hugging me. My father never hugged me. I realized how devastating this was for me. I had no healthy touch experience from my parents within my childhood memories to the present. I clearly remember fantasizing, as a young child, about my dad's friends holding me and having sexual fantasies about them. I was not getting healthy touch from anyone.

I believed that the only time one touched was for sex, so I would dread any touch by anyone, as it would lead to sex. Mentoring sessions, where healthy men and women held me safely, brought incredible healing and my biggest breakthrough. I felt like a little child being loved by a parent in a very healthy way. I discovered quickly that I *could* get healthy touch. I knew that I had been seeking touch with men in an unhealthy way. I just wanted to experience affection and had used sex to get it.

Memory work of the inner child was also another key factor in my transitioning. When Richard asked me to draw pictures with my non-dominant hand and write down feelings and experiences, I truly thought this was a crazy and a stupid task. However, I quickly had clear memories of childhood. It came out on paper about how I left myself wide open for inappropriate touch by one relative and sexual abuse by teenage boys who would baby-sit and take me on outings. This helped to peel away more layers of what had felt like, "I'm gay."

Group therapy sessions, with people who were working towards healing, were incredibly helpful. It was another key to my healing to have a support network and individuals with whom I could say whatever I needed to say. Sometimes it was to tell them how I was healing or to tell them I was having a bad time and felt like acting out. It could be to tell them I had sexual feelings for another person in the group, and to discuss why those feelings were there and how to resolve them in a healthy way.

My pastor is a great friend and very secure in his heterosexuality. We get together to talk about anything and everything. He is a great mentor. We go to the gym, play tennis, get together for lunch, and just hang out. I am totally comfortable with him in a real friendship.

Massage therapy really helped me to accept appropriate touch. Having deep pressure applied to my muscles felt as if my body was transitioning from sexual touch to the acceptance of normal, healthy touch.

In July 1995, I started a therapy course that changed my life. I had individual therapy, sometimes twice a week, for a little less than two years. I was in a support group for the same amount of time. At the end of this time, it became apparent that I was living a wonderful, productive life with my wife, children, and friends. I had and have the tools necessary to continue to grow as the man I have become. My darkness and anxiety are completely gone. I really enjoy sex with my wife. I no longer have sexual attractions for men. I am not, nor ever was, gay. I had addictive homo-emotional feelings for men. I feel fantastic because I had a choice made available to me. I believe strongly that I had to make a choice for *me*, and it was a choice I believe in. I chose to transition, and *change is possible.*

I no longer identify with the man I was before July 1995. That was a lifetime ago. I feel reborn. At the beginning of my therapy, I felt so alone. A friend in my support group said, "If you think you're alone, then you are wrong. You are not alone anymore." I have God, my wife, my two children, and the great prospects of what life holds for me each day!

Conclusion

Here are some of the causes of Christian's SSA:

1. There was insufficient bonding between Christian and his father, therefore he was unable to incorporate his dad's masculinity and feel his own maleness. As Christian mentioned, he never recalled being held or touched by his dad. This created a deep wound in his soul and need for male affection and attention.

2. There was some connection with his mother, but not as much as he needed. This increased his desire for physical affection, which was later to be used and confused through sexual abuse.

3. Christian's temperament was highly sensitive in a relatively insensitive environment. His love needs went unmet and unnoticed.

4. Christian recalled numerous experiences of childhood sexual abuse by men and boys in the neighborhood. This created a pattern of sexualizing his need for paternal and fraternal intimacy. From that time, Christian used sex to obtain some form of male affection.

5. Like many men and women in their forties, unresolved issues of the past begin to manifest during this stage of life, often called a "mid-life crisis." Our shadow self, or unconscious parts, manifest in present-day life through unwanted desires or behaviors. Christian, though married to his loving wife, would act out sexually with other men. This was a means whereby his wounded self, those unconscious issues repressed for many years, worked to get Christian's attention in order to resolve his past.

Suggestions

How family and friends can help men like Christian:

1. I can't say it often enough: Fathers, *please* bond with your sons by showing them your affection, attention and affirmation. Mothers, *please* bond with your daughters by displaying appropriate physical affection, and participate in their activities. Dads join in your son's world, and moms be engaged in your daughter's world. Grandfathers and uncles bless the lives of your grandsons and nephews. Grandmothers and aunts bless the lives of your granddaughters and nieces.

2. Christian learned to sexualize his need for male affection and attention after being sexually abused as a child. In the process of healing, it was imperative for him to experience closeness with heterosexual men who were not interested in any form of sexual activity. This was a great healing for Christian. Three healthy, heterosexual men stood in the gap for me as well, helping me heal the many years that I learned to sexualize the legitimate need for healthy male bonding.

3. Mentor someone like Christian, who never experienced healthy paternal/fraternal affection. If an adult had offered this to him as a child, he never would have had to sexualize that desire. Men, reach out to those who experience SSA, let them know that you care, whether or not they wish to live a homosexual life or seek change. Women, reach out to women who experience SSA, and show them healthy feminine love, sans the sex. What their heart of hearts is calling out for is acceptance and healthy affection. Men, be a brother, a friend, a mentor. Women, be a sister, a friend, a mentor. In the process, you will change someone's life. I also know that such a beautiful man or woman will enrich your life.

Chapter Three

Clues as to Why Five Celebrities Experience SSA

	Why I Believe They Have SSA								
	1 Lack of bonding with same-sex parent	2 Over-attached to / or wounded by opposite-sex parent	3 Hypersensitivity	4 Sibling wounds	5 Sexual abuse	6 Body-image wounds	7 Same-sex peer wounds	8 Adoption or death of a parent	9 Socialization into "gay" mythology
Greg Louganis	√	√	√			√	√	√	√
Melissa Etheridge	√	√	√	√	√	√	√		√
John Amaechi	√	√	√			√	√		√
Rosie O'Donnell	√	√	√		√	√	√	√	√
Kevin Jennings	√	√	√	√		√	√	√	√

© Richard Cohen, M.A., 2022

All these men and women have similar causes for their SSA, further demonstrating that same-sex attraction is an acquired condition.

- Greg Louganis—Olympic gold medalist diver
- Melissa Ethridge—Singer, songwriter
- John Amaechi—Retired NBA basketball player
- Rosie O'Donnell—Comedienne, actress, talk-show host
- Kevin Jennings—Former U.S. Department of Education/ Founder of GLSEN

LGBTQ+ activists fought long and hard to redefine SSA as "gay." Why? Because the word "gay" means happy. Remember, someone who adopts a gay identity has accepted the "born this way and cannot change" myth, while others who experience unwanted SSA do not take on such an identity. With the socialization of the gay paradigm, homosexuality has become legitimized and public opinion has changed. This makes it possible for those who have only felt prejudice and rejection to experience love and acceptance. As we learned in the seven stages of "coming out," many men and women who experience SSA adopted a gay identity in order to feel some semblance of self-worth and pride after feeling like outcasts for much of their lives. We have also learned that no one is essentially born with SSA, but everywhere we turn we hear: "I was born gay, it's who I am. I've felt this way since I was a child." Oprah and other celebrities continue to affirm homosexuality without ever looking behind the curtain to see what's there.

In this chapter, let us look at the background of five celebrities in the USA who define themselves as gay or lesbian. As we consider their experiences and family dynamics, I think you will notice familiar patterns emerging. I have summarized these similarities in the above chart. By observing their experiences and family dynamics, we will observe that:

- **No one is essentially born with SSA**
- **No one simply chooses to have SSA**
- **Change is possible**

> *Throughout each of these evaluations, a summary of the celebrity's life experiences appears in italics, interwoven with my own perspective, analysis and comments. I would have preferred to incorporate more direct quotes from each author; however, most of their publishers were not forthcoming with permission. Therefore, I have used their words sparingly.* Direct quotes appear inside quotation marks and are not in italics.

Greg Louganis

Greg Louganis is one of the most celebrated divers of our time. He is a six-time World Champion with four gold medals at the Olympics and 47 National Championship titles. He also experiences SSA and is living with AIDS. Mr. Louganis is a brave, persistent and extremely sensitive man. He developed homosexual feelings through no fault of his own. As you will see in this evaluation, it is apparent how Greg's SSA developed. Throughout his life, as detailed in his autobiography Breaking the Surface, *he battled with depression and low self-worth.* All quotes are taken from his book (page numbers are in parenthesis).

Dr. Joseph Nicolosi, Sr., a leading psychologist in the field of sexual orientation therapy, describes the triadic relationship of a sensitive boy detached from his father and over-attached to his mother. Greg fits this profile to a tee. In Greg's own words, you may observe the many causes of his SSA that were identified in Chapter Two. All of these early experiences resulted in substance abuse, same-sex attraction, and abusive homosexual relationships.

"What you will read here is the story of a lonely boy who struggled with dyslexia and discrimination, yet discovered he had a great gift for acrobatics and diving. It's about a shy kid who battled low self-esteem, bouts of depression, and conflicts over his sexuality yet still went on to become one of the most accomplished divers of all time" (*Breaking the Surface,* Greg Louganis with Eric Marcus, Sourcebooks, Naperville, IL, 2006, pp. viii-ix).

Throughout Greg's autobiography, we observe the many risk factors for his SSA:

1 – Hypersensitive temperament and low self-worth
2 – Detachment from his abusive father
3 – Over-attachment to his mother
4 – Abuse by male peers
5 – Body-image wounds
6 – Adoption

HYPERSENSITIVE TEMPERAMENT / LOW SELF-WORTH

Greg was hypersensitive. He never felt strong enough to stand up for himself, and therefore internalized all the negative messages he received from within and outside of himself. Greg felt rejected by his biological parents, adoptive father and male peers. Depression was a major issue throughout his life. He attempted suicide three times. His self-worth was always tied to his diving. We call this performance-based behavior, whereby one tries to gain acceptance and love through one's activities and achievements.

Acrobatics and diving provided relief from his difficult childhood. He questioned if his adoptive parents really loved him; meanwhile the kids at school were beating him up. He felt absolutely hopeless.

Greg experienced dyslexia from an early age and was put into a special education class, as his teachers didn't understand his learning disability. From 12 years of age, he was miserable, felt isolated from the other kids, and hated his physical appearance. His self-perception was "terrible." He believed that no one could understand him, a common experience for many young children who experience SSA. Throughout his formative years, Greg "played negative messages" over and over again in his head—no one wanted him, no one really cared about him, and he was deeply flawed. Greg was also called "sissy," "fag," and other hurtful names by kids at school. It made him feel "worthless," like he had no right to be alive. Being so shy and withdrawn, he didn't feel worthy of acceptance by his peers, so he used diving to attain self-worth.

DETACHMENT FROM HIS ABUSIVE DAD

Greg's relationship with his father was fractured. He developed a defensive detachment (an emotional wall of separation) toward his dad at a very young age. His father was authoritative, stoic, unaffectionate, and an alcoholic. Greg's deep homo-emotional wound laid the groundwork for his future same-sex attraction.

Greg became close to his father during the latter years of his life, when his dad was diagnosed with cancer. Even though their relationship improved, the devastating wounds of Greg's childhood were not healed.

"Mom said that Dad was born an angry man. Dad wasn't the type of father who would give you a hug and say that he loved you. He was stoic and, except for anger, not very good at expressing his emotions" (28). *The family walked around "on eggshells," not to upset their dad or he would become enraged while drinking. This was the norm in the Louganis household. By the time Greg was twelve or thirteen years old, they would simply sit in silence during dinner. He ran away from home at times when his Dad drank and threatened to beat him.*

Greg's father didn't like his dancing and acrobatics, and did not attend any of his performances. Because the kids at school were constantly labeling him "sissy" and "faggot," Greg internalized the same negative messages from his father. On the other hand, his dad was overly involved with Greg's diving activities. Greg thought his father's involvement in his diving was more about himself than about Greg.

OVER-ATTACHMENT TO HIS MOTHER

Greg's maternal grandfather was an alcoholic, just like his dad. Greg's mom was unable to have children, so they adopted Despina two years before they adopted Greg. As with many SSA men, Greg was extremely

97

close to his mother and quite distant from his father. Being a hypersensitive boy, he more easily connected to women. Throughout Greg's life, he continued his very special and close relationship with his mother, typical of most SSA men.

Fathers pay attention! When you have a sensitive and gifted son, be sure to join in his world and then bring him into yours. As I described in Chapter Two, the first critical bonding time that is essential for the healthy development of a boy's sense of masculinity, is from the ages of 1½ to 3 years old. During this period of time the boy learns to walk and talk. He then needs to separate from his mother and identify with his own gender role model, his dad, or a substitute father figure. If this does not happen, then the boy will continue to gender identify with his mother.

Some researchers and therapists believe this factor is one reason there are more SSA men than SSA women, because girls, even though they too will differentiate and individuate from their mothers, will continue to gender identify with her. The boys have this extra developmental task— separating from mom and bonding with dad—which is why fathers are so important for their sons during this and other developmental stages. The good news for dads of SSA sons is that you can restore the relationship with your adolescent or adult son at anytime (of course, the same holds true for moms with SSA daughters). It is never too late to heal! (Please read Gay Children, Straight Parents: A Plan for Family Healing *for the "how to's" of reconnecting with your children who experience SSA.)*

Greg's mom made all his costumes for acrobatics and attended all his performances, unlike his dad who stayed away entirely. She was also supportive of his diving and didn't pressure him, only wanting Greg to be happy.

"If Dad got mad, she usually just shut up. She said she didn't want to give him any excuse to do anything. Mom learned from being with her dad that you don't talk back to a drunk. That's how she learned to keep the peace. Unfortunately, that's how I learned, too" (30).

ABUSE BY MALE PEERS

Greg was passive in relationships with tough boys. He learned this pattern of behavior from his mother, his primary role model and source of love. From her, he learned to keep his mouth shut, to keep the peace at all costs. This cost Greg dearly, especially in a relationship later on with Tom, his abusive partner of six years.

When Greg was ten, he was in a very bad fight. A kid punched him and slammed his head into the asphalt until he bled. His father witnessed the entire episode without intervening. "He might as well have been the one throwing the punches. That he would be there and not help me was so terrible that I blocked it from my memory. All I remembered was the fight itself and feeling that my father thought I deserved what I got" (36).

Greg didn't know how to stand up for himself, as his father never taught him how to do so. Greg also had a distorted view of himself and others because of being disconnected from his father, male peers, and ultimately, himself. Greg used his diving to gain affection, attention, and affirmation from others—again, performance-based behavior—seeking love and approval through his achievements.

It bears repeating that this never works because children need to be loved for who they are, not for what they do. Adults who use their talents and abilities to gain acceptance are often internally troubled, avoiding their core pain and wounds.

Home life was horrific for Greg, and so was school. He found no refuge anywhere except through acrobatics and diving. From the very first day of elementary school, the kids called him names because of his dark, Samoan complexion. Then came the derogatory comments, "faggot," "sissy," and more. Unfortunately, when Greg went to his teacher for support, she did nothing. This led Greg to believe that something was wrong with him.

From third grade on, Greg got beat up a lot, especially by the rough kids at the bus stop and in the school cafeteria. He would tell them he didn't want to fight, or, "I know you can kick my ass, so why bother?" Then they would call me a 'sissy-boy faggot'" (34).

Greg had no close friends at school, and never had a "best friend." He was constantly being beaten up, and even the girls cheered the bullies on. Greg internalized all these experiences, thinking that the kids were right and he was wrong, and that he somehow deserved to be treated abusively.

BODY-IMAGE WOUNDS

Greg was detached from his physical appearance, which is common among same-sex attracted individuals. Once someone detaches from their primary gender role model, in this case Greg's father, and once he detaches from his same-sex peers, then he rejects his own sense of masculinity, gender identity, and physical appearance, as if to say, "I don't want to be like dad or the other guys." He then spends the rest of his life looking for that unattained self-acceptance and love in the arms of other SSA men. However, it never works very well because both are looking for the same thing, and it's something that neither one of them has experienced: the fullness of their own masculinity and gender identity. As you will soon learn, this is quite evident in the lives of Melissa Etheridge, Rosie O'Donnell, John Amaechi, Kevin Jennings and most SSA men and women.

Greg became known as a sex icon after his first Olympics, but internally he still felt like an outcast. People continued to shower Greg with compliments about his handsome appearance; however, due to low self-esteem he couldn't receive their flattering remarks.

ADOPTION

Adoption was yet another source of rejection for this highly sensitive boy. The core belief of feeling abandoned was a great source of pain throughout Greg's life—rejected by his biological parents, by his adoptive father, and by his male peers.

The first nine months of his life, Greg lived with a foster family. His biological father was Samoan and his biological mother was a blond-haired, blue-eyed Northern European, like his adoptive mother.

Eventually Greg accepted the love of his adoptive parents in spite of the trauma he experienced with them. "But the emotional damage had already been done, and I've struggled throughout my life with trusting whether anyone genuinely cared for me" (43).

SUBSTANCE ABUSE

While in school, Greg smoked cigarettes and marijuana, used other drugs, and drank alcohol to anesthetize his pain. Eventually he stopped smoking and drinking, but he continued to use pills until he began therapy in his thirties.

Greg started smoking "pot" to fit in with the smart kids at school because he always felt that he didn't measure up to their intellectual prowess. Greg drank a six-pack of beer each day for many years.

SUBSTITUTE DADS (DIVING COACHES)

John Anders was Greg's second diving coach. Greg envied John's sons because he wanted an emotionally warm and available father like John. Mr. Anders spent time with his kids, something Greg's father never did, and thus Greg always felt like a "bother" to his dad. Through his relationship with Mr. Anders, for the first time in his life, Greg felt cared for by a male authority figure.

In January of 1976, Greg moved in with his third diving coach, Dr. Lee. Although Greg "loved" Mrs. Lee, he transferred onto Dr. Lee similar feelings and responses he had for his own father, perceiving Dr. Lee as "stoic," "stern" and "cold." He wished Dr. Lee had been more like John Anders, who was the "fantasy father" of Greg's dreams.

Greg grew very close with Mrs. Lee, once again typical behavior for many boys who experience SSA—close to female authority figures, distant and detached from male figures. They feel more comfortable in the world of women and detached from the world of men. Mr. Lee's harsh character served to make Greg further withdraw into himself.

Greg's next and final coach, Ron O'Brien, was more like John Anders. He helped Greg feel more secure, building up his sense of self-worth. "He was more nurturing…" (89). *Greg found out in 1987 that he was HIV positive. He shared this with Coach O'Brien, who was very loving and supportive. Greg had to take medication every four hours. Ron said,* "We'll get through this together" (178). *However, despite Ron's positive support of Greg, he still harbored the pain experienced from his dad and male peers. Time doesn't heal all wounds. They only fester until we deal with them.*

HOMOSEXUAL RELATIONSHIPS

Greg experienced a conflict in his soul. I believe that every person who experiences SSA initially goes through this stage. Everyone's conscience knows that sexual relationships between those of the same sex are inherently incongruent with natural law. Because Greg never successfully connected and bonded with his dad and same-sex peers, he longed to be loved by men. This is a natural desire of every child. Those core love needs must be met in the critical years of child development; otherwise after puberty, they will look for love through sexual relationships. What were once legitimate needs for male bonding then become eroticized after adolescence. Greg wanted to be held and feel safe, which he never experienced with his father or male peers. If only he had received the right kind of support and love from men who understood the meaning of his SSA, he would never have had to experience so much heartache and pain in abusive homosexual relationships.

Greg had a crush on a Soviet diver at his first Olympics in 1976. This man held and caressed him, and Greg said that he "wanted to stay" in his arms forever…the longing of a child for his father's love. As far as Greg shared in his book, there was no real sexual relationship between the two of them, just cuddling and being close. Greg recalled being attracted to men from the time he was 7-8 years old. He was confused about these attractions, but after being held by this diver, he longed to be held again by a man.

When Greg was 16, he had his first sexual experience with a man who was in his thirties. Greg enjoyed the sex while it occurred, but felt guilty afterwards. He just wanted to be physically close and "held." At that time in his life, Greg believed that sex between two men was sinful, according to his faith.

Greg had three short-term boyfriends followed by a six-year relationship with Tom, and then a four-year relationship with Steven. His first boyfriend was Daniel. It was a very unhealthy and co-dependent relationship. Next was Jeff, who had sexual relations with women throughout their relationship. His third boyfriend was Kevin. They got into arguments and physical altercations, beating on each other. Greg transferred his tremendous need for love and acceptance onto his male partners, that which he did not experience from his dad or male peers. This creates an emotional time warp, re-enacting the father-son relationship, trying to get a man to love him; however, the core issue was his need for male bonding and acceptance.

Greg began dating Tom in 1982. They moved in together after the 1984 Olympics. They were together for six years.

As Harville Hendrix states in his book, Getting the Love You Want (Henry Holt and Company, New York, 2008), "Each of us enters adulthood harboring unresolved childhood issues with our parents, whether or not we know it or will admit it. Those needs have to be met, because their satisfaction is equated, in our unconscious minds, with survival. Therefore, their satisfaction becomes the agenda in adult love relationships" (p. 26).

Tom was taller than Greg, had "broad shoulders" and a "good-size" chest" and was five years older (Greg was 22 when they started dating). Greg's memories of his time with Tom were "too painful to recall," and that he is "embarrassed" by what he let Tom do to him during their six years together.

Tom was quite logical, like Greg's dad, as well as eloquent, always in charge. He did almost everything for Greg, making him feel totally cared for: "This was my fantasy: to be loved and taken care of. And I loved

Tom all the more because he showered me with so much attention" (134). *Again, Greg is like a little boy searching for his father's love and acceptance in the arms of his boyfriend. He thought he had struck gold in finding Tom, but in reality he was partnered with another abusive father figure.*

Before they moved in together, Greg dated other men. When Tom found out, he went crazy, demanding that Greg call each of the men he had seen, and tell them he was sorry and couldn't see them again. Greg felt humiliated, and once again, like the boys who beat him up, Greg felt responsible, that everything was his fault (even though he and Tom were not in an exclusive relationship when he dated those men). Following the phone calls, Tom became "enraged," took a large kitchen knife, grabbed Greg's neck and raped him. Simultaneously, he berated Greg using disgusting words. Greg cried and begged Tom to stop. Tom told Greg that he deserved this. After everything was over, it was Greg who apologized for hurting Tom! This was not the only time that Tom would prove to be violent in their relationship.

Tom told Greg that he wasn't getting big endorsements because he was too feminine…more put-downs. It made Greg doubt himself and feel guilty, even though he was financially supporting both of them. Tom's rules according to Greg: Don't ever bother him when he's on the phone; he has to win all games; Greg serves him all his meals; he controls all of Greg's schedule; he showed almost no affection after living together; and Greg couldn't ask questions about his late night outings. Years later, Greg found out that all through their relationship, while Tom accused Greg of being unfaithful, Tom was a prostitute, hustling on Santa Monica Boulevard! Can you imagine how shocked and shameful Greg felt when he learned of this?

As you can see, Tom was treating Greg in the same manner that Greg's father had treated his mother. And he reacted to Tom in similar ways as his mother had reacted to his father. He was re-living the dynamics of his parent's relationship. His inner child, so desperate for his father's love, was trying to change the abuser Tom, who represented his dad. This never works, as Greg eventually discovered. "All I really wanted from Tom was for him to love me and to show me affection, but he was never the kind of man you would describe as loving or affectionate" (159). *Eventually, Greg stood up to Tom and asked him to move out. Tom threatened Greg with blackmail, to reveal his homosexuality to the press and speak slanderous things about him. Finally, they reached a settlement where Greg would support him for the rest of his life (as Tom was living with AIDS by that time). Tom remained abusive toward Greg until the end. He passed away in 1989, the same year Greg's father died! Greg then met Steven. They were together for four years before splitting up. Greg is still living with HIV/AIDS.*

CONCLUSION

Perhaps now you can better understand the life of Olympic gold medalist Greg Louganis. It is amazing what he has been through. He practiced diving five to six hours daily, year after year, while internally suffering. The greatest pain in my heart about Greg is that he should never have suffered like this. Greg's child-like need for male affection could have been satisfied in healthy, non-sexual relationships with heterosexual men.

Following are suggestions for Greg and men who experience SSA like him:

1. *Instead of sex, Greg needed male mentors to help heal his father wounds. Ron was a wonderful coach for Greg; however, Greg needed to grieve the many losses of his past. Like most children of alcoholics, Greg didn't openly express his feelings and needs to Ron and others while growing up. If you see a young boy whose father has rejected him, put your arm around him, show him healthy masculine love, and allow him to grieve the many losses he has experienced in his life.*

   When I was presenting the basic causes of SSA at a conference many years ago, the soundman approached me after the talk. He stated, "You just described my life. However, my base-ball coach literally put his arm around me and became the dad I never had. Without him, I know that I would have ended up developing homosexual feelings. He saved my life!"

2. *The unspoken rule in the alcoholic family system is that no one is allowed to have their own thoughts, feelings, or needs. Greg's mother, the enabler or codependent, did her best to keep the peace, and to keep the children from upsetting dad. One reason Greg threw himself into aerobics and then diving was to medicate his pain. Eventually he began to drink and use drugs to further anesthetize his wounds. Greg needed to get in touch with himself and heal his wounds; however he used sex to obtain some male affection and attention, which he never experienced from his father or male peers.*

    When you see a child stuck in an alcoholic family system, do your best to suggest that the entire family seek help. Greg's mother followed the pattern of her mother. Greg followed his mother's pattern. The chain needed to be broken. Outside inter-vention is often necessary in this type of situation.

3. *If you see such a sensitive boy in school, on the swim team, any-where in your community, please stop others from teasing him. Bullying is wrong all of the time, regardless of the child's nature. No one stood up for Greg, not his own father, none of the kids at school, or any teachers or administrators. Stand up and stop the bullying. Greg and others like him deserve to be treated with respect.*

4. *Boys who are too close to their mothers and distant or detached from their fathers need someone to intercede. SSA can be pre-vented. If you see a relative or close friend in this situation, gently speak to the parents. Parents love their kids, but sometimes they need a gentle nudge from an observer to help set love in order.*

Melissa Etheridge

"What I really am is this little girl looking for acceptance. Looking for love and trying to fill up this hole inside of me that has always been empty" (*The Truth Is ... My Life in Love and Music*, Melissa Etheridge with Laura Morton, Random House, New York, 2002, p. xiv). "I was tortured by my need for love and affection—my need to find someone who could fill up the emptiness inside me. I'm still driven by that need as a songwriter" (31).

Melissa Etheridge, a celebrated rock singer who won an Oscar, multiple Grammy Awards, and other accolades from the music industry, is beautifully transparent in her autobiography The Truth Is ... My Life in Love and Music. *I deeply admire her passion, authenticity, and vulnerability, baring her soul throughout this tell-all autobiography. She recalls childhood experiences in Kansas, beginning with a painful birth, a cold and disapproving mother, the sexual and physical abuse of her older sister, rejection by same-sex peers, and finding acceptance only through her father. Within Melissa's family there was no expression of emotion; it was a cold and unsafe place for her as a child and adolescent. She was born on her older sister Jennifer's birthday, which created a lifetime of rivalry for attention and for what little affection was available within their family. Jennifer, who was four years older than Melissa, sexually and physically abused her from the time she was 6 through age 11, instilling within Melissa a psychological and neurological pattern of intimacy with women which involved sexual behavior. Music became Melissa's refuge, a safe place of comfort and solace. Her dad supported her pursuit of music and her SSA, while her mother was disapproving of both. Unable to bond or identify with her mother, Melissa modeled herself after her only real source of love, her father. Throughout Melissa's life, she sought refuge in the arms of many abusive and unavailable women, who were similar to her mom and Jennifer. This type of behavior is characteristic of many* women who experience SSA, transferring onto their partners a child's need for acceptance and love.

I believe that Melissa Etheridge may experience SSA because of the following factors:

1 – Insufficient mother-daughter bonding
2 – Over identification with her father
3 – Sexual and physical abuse by her older sister
4 – Abusive same-sex relationships
5 – Gender dis-identification: feeling more masculine than feminine

MOTHER WOUND

Melissa's birth, on May 29, 1961, in Leavenworth, Kansas, was terribly painful. Her mother went into labor at home. When they got to the hospital, the doctor was on break, so the nurses held Melissa in for 15 minutes. Her birth experience felt crushing to Melissa, as she was born "black-and-blue and bruised." Her family never spoke about this, or any other important matters of the heart. Melissa felt that she was physically and symbolically bruised from the time of her birth.

Melissa's mother did not communicate with her; they had quite a distant relationship. On the other hand, Melissa loved her grandmother who lived in Arkansas. It was the only positive and nurturing female relationship she had during her formative years. Melissa felt appreciated, accepted, and loved by her grandmother, but not by her mother. She felt unconditional love for the first time in her life. Melissa's grandmother died when she was in the sixth grade, and typical of her family, there was no expression of emotion or grief, even at the funeral. After this loss, Melissa shut down emotionally and expressed her feelings through her music.

When her mother found out about Melissa's homosexuality, she was cold and rejecting. She wrote her daughter a letter telling of her disapproval, which deeply hurt Melissa. They never discussed it again. As an adult, Melissa never felt accepted by her mother. Melissa experienced a profound wounding in her heart because she never sufficiently bonded with her mother, who should have been her primary role model of femininity. As we will see, Melissa spent many years of her life moving from one relationship to the other, seeking to experience the femininity she never internalized, and a mother's love and acceptance never felt.

IDENTIFICATION WITH FATHER AND MASCULINITY

Melissa's father was supportive of her music. Her dad bought her first guitar, drove her to band practice and performances. She was much closer to her father than her mother, which is typical for many women who experience SSA. Melissa internalized his masculinity, being more identified with him and dis-identified with her mom and the femininity that she represented. "I was very much a tomboy, completely awkward in my body. My mother never showed me how to do my hair, how to dress 'right.'" (6).

Melissa's appearance seems to be more masculine than feminine, as she modeled herself after her father, who was her primary source of love during the formative years of her life. When she revealed her homosexuality to her father, he was completely accepting and supportive, unlike her mom who was both rejecting and judgmental. "My whole life I'd wanted to be like my dad" (126).

SIBLING WOUND / SEXUAL ABUSE

From the time Melissa was six years old, Jennifer began to systematically and repeatedly sexually and physically abuse her. Jennifer would first speak sweetly to Melissa, and then give her directions how to "touch" her…inappropriately. Afterwards Melissa felt both horrible and shameful. Following the family code, there was never any discussion or sharing about what transpired. As this continued, Melissa began to disconnect, or dissociate from her body, just being an "observer" to what occurred. This phenomenon is called "psychic splitting," common among those who experience sexual abuse. The individual feels too much pain, and detaches from her body. Some may even feel that they rise above their bodies when being abused, observing what is taking place, because the pain is just too great to contain.

Jennifer became increasingly manipulative and angrier toward Melissa as she grew, tormenting her with acts of abuse and violence, like slapping across the face for no apparent reason. Randomly, she would scream and frighten her. Two of Jennifer's behaviors—manipulation and controlling—are traits that Melissa says she finds attractive in women, especially ones she is romantically involved with. Dr. Harville Hendix, again in his book Getting the Love You Want, *calls this the unconscious marriage, being attracted to someone who carries the negative characteristics of our caregivers/siblings, and then trying to change the person in order to obtain the love so desperately wanted and needed as a child.*

After the physical and sexual abuse ended when Melissa was 11 and Jennifer 15, Melissa began to eat in order to numb the feelings of emptiness and pain. She tried to fill the "hole" inside with food, movies, and music. It was the only time that she felt safe and comforted, escaping into the world of make believe and "fairy tales." This is typical behavior of children who experience abuse, a defensive reaction to dull the pain, to medicate themselves, not knowing how to reconcile the contradictions in their lives.

ABUSIVE SAME-SEX RELATIONSHIPS

Melissa was needy because of the coldness she experienced from her mother and sexual and physical abuse by her sister. While growing up, Melissa found no one to share with about her heartaches and pain. In her sophomore year of high school, she became intimate with Jane, who began to act like Jennifer, slapping Melissa across the face for no reason. A cycle of intimacy and abuse became a repetitive pattern in many of Melissa's adult relationships with women.

"I'm trying to get from other people what they are simply not capable of giving to me. Wanting it. Needing it. Craving it. Obsessing over it. But never attaching the concept of ever receiving it" (34). *Melissa was well-known for her "one-night stands," sleeping around with many women. She would seduce them, win them over, and then leave them. This was her addictive relationship pattern for many years.*

Melissa enjoyed the feeling of conquest, but she always withheld herself from them.

Melissa went from one relationship to the next, attempting to fill the emptiness in her soul and resolve the painful relationships with her mother and sister. It never worked. She kept drawing to herself women who were emotionally unavailable, one after another. Then she met and moved in with Julie, actor Lou Diamond Phillips's ex-wife, and they had two children. For a while they became poster women for the LGBTQ+ community, appearing on the cover of Newsweek *and interviewed by 20/20. Over the years, their relationship became increasingly strained for numerous reasons and eventually they broke up.*

"She [Julie] so represented my mother to me—that same distant and aloof attitude ... I just felt so left out, so lost and confused" (140). *One of Melissa's most popular songs, "Come To My Window," is about her emotional pain regarding Julie. After twelve years together, Julie decided that she was not a lesbian, announcing, "I'm not gay!" Melissa was devastated. This type of behavior is common among some women who experience SSA. Their sexuality seems to be more fluid, with some reverting back to heterosexuality.*

In April 2003, Melissa was engaged to actress Tammy Michaels. They married in Malibu, CA in September 2003. Their wedding was featured on ABC's InStyle Celebrity Weddings. In October 2006, Tammy had twins, a boy and a girl. In April 2010, Melissa and Tammy broke up. These types of relationship often fail to work out because both partners are looking for the same thing, which neither one of them has experienced: a successful bond with their mothers and a secure sense of their own feminine gender identity.

CONCLUSION

"This was supposed to be the time of my life. I had made it as a rock star. I had a big house, a fancy sports car, and a relationship that was a lot of work. I guess I expected all of that to fill the big, dark, empty black hole in my heart … I thought that when I became a famous rock star, all of my problems would fade away. That's why I wanted to be famous in the first place: to solve my problems. I thought that being loved and adored by millions of people would surely fill up that deep, endless pit I carry inside myself. I thought that I wouldn't be starved for that attention, affection, or redemption if I had the love of millions. But I was. I was still emotionally malnourished" (182-183).

This reveals Melissa's "truth" about her life. Just as Greg Louganis had done, Melissa used performance-based behaviors in an attempt to fill the "empty black hole" in her soul. She used her rock star status, her relationships with women, and the many accolades she's received over the years. None of these things worked.

This is the pain of so many men and women who experience SSA. They are looking for unattained love in the arms of other men or women—desperately seeking to fill their need for parental and peer bonding. Melissa never experienced the nurturing touch and care of her mom, was repeatedly sexually and physically abused by her older sister, and was attached to her only source of love and acceptance in the family, her dad, who became her gender role model. It is easy to observe why Melissa Etheridge developed SSA, and how it continues to play out in her life.

Here are some suggestions for healing that may help Melissa and other women with similar issues:

1. *Melissa needed a warm, maternal mother's love, affection, and support. If Melissa had come to know other warm-hearted women like her grandmother, who would have doted on her, showed her the ways of women, taught her how to dress, helped her do her hair, taken her out, and most of all simply loved her for who she was, she would have had a very different life.*

2. *Melissa was drawn to abusive relationships with women, mirroring Jennifer and her mother's treatment. Some women who experienced sexual abuse, and who didn't sufficiently bond with their same-sex parent, learned to substitute sex for intimacy. Melissa needed healthy female peers to embrace her, demonstrating healthy feminine love.*

   If you are a heterosexual woman, and you know another woman who experiences SSA and was sexually abused, chances are she didn't bond successfully with her mother and/or same-sex peers. Please stand in the gap for her. Wrap your arms around her. If she sexually comes on to you, she's just doing what she was taught to do as a child. Hold her hands and look into her eyes and gently say, "I love you and I don't need that from you." Then give her a warm hug. What a new message of hope and acceptance she will receive, a gift of love never experienced before in her life!

3. *Melissa Etheridge and Rosie O'Donnell, as well as many other men and women who experience SSA, go from relationship to relationship. They are seeking that unattained parental and peer love. If you have experienced love from your parents and/or other mentors in your life, then please be the giver of the gift of love to men or women who experience SSA. Women like Melissa need your love and affection. You will become the solution to the homosexual dilemma!*

John Amaechi

Former National Basketball Association (NBA) player John Amaechi is another example of how a boy may develop SSA, as described in his auto-biography Man in the Middle *(ESPN Books, New York City, 2007), and in an interview from* The Advocate *(a LGBTQ+ magazine). John lacked positive male role models while growing up. His father left the family when John was just a little boy. He, his mother, and two sisters fled from Boston, MA to Manchester, England in order to escape his father's abusive threats. John's dad followed them with repeated attempts to kid-nap his children. Meanwhile, John's maternal grandfather was verbally abusive and critical of John throughout his childhood.*

John's "Mum" acted as mother and father, his source of love and pro-tection, his primary role model. His maternal Grandmother was another source of healthy feminine love. John was also close to his two sisters. But from his male peers at school, John experienced rejection, name-calling, and incessant mockery for his physical appearance and lack of athletic prowess. As a young boy, John was overweight and non-athletic. He ate to numb his pain, and was called a "whale" by the other boys in swim class. Like other men who experience SSA, John was a hypersensitive boy. He was quite introverted and preferred to spend his quiet time alone reading. It was in these solitary times that he found solace. His "Mum" worked very hard, managing two jobs, caring for others through her medical practice.

In my estimation, John Amaechi's SSA is a result of:

1 – Profound father wound
2 – Persistently abusive grandfather
3 – Overattachment to mother
4 – Hypersensitive temperament
5 – Body-image wounds
6 – Male peer wounds

John experienced father, grandfather, and male peer rejection, exces-sive female attention, and a hypersensitive temperament. Due to these factors, he was unable to navigate his way in the world of men. From the age of 17, as a 6' 8" teenager living in England, John was discovered by a basketball scout. Through intense practice and excellent coaching, for the first time in his life, John began to gain a feeling of being valued. Finally, he felt a sense of belonging and acceptance amongst his male peers. Basketball increased John's self-esteem. Until then, he had been a fatherless, "overweight," sensitive, non-athletic "misfit" and "nerd." Unfortunately, John never dealt with the core wounds that created his SSA, never reconciling his father, grandfather, and male peer wounds. This became more apparent when reading John's account of his relationships with men in the NBA, how awkward and ill at ease he was with the other players. To this day, John does not like his body and keeps his shirt on while in the presence of others. This is the direct result of internalizing all the derogatory names he heard while in gym and swim class.

Like Greg Louganis and Melissa Etheridge, John Amaechi used his basketball talent as a performance-based behavior to gain acceptance and love. As we've seen, this never works because the "inner child" doesn't want to be accepted for what he does, *but for who he* is. *John received lots of attention for his basketball talent, but still the little boy within seeks the unattained paternal and fraternal love. When sex enters into this equation through homosexual relationships, it prevents the child within from experiencing unconditional love.*

In my opinion, John's SSA grew from the aforementioned experiences, as well as his inborn temperament of hypersensitivity. Because the world does not understand the true meaning of SSA, John was led to believe that he was born gay. John is an intelligent, sensitive, and insightful man. He was never offered correct information about why he experienced homosexual desires. John is a man of great character, values and tenacity. His mother, "Mum," as he called her, instilled within him a tremendous work ethic and respect for all human life. As a medical doctor, she was an excellent role model, giving of herself for the sake of others. John acquired her sense of public service, offering his free time while in the NBA, to mentor at-risk teenage boys.

Someday, I would like to sit down with John and share ideas, opinions, and thoughts. Today he is a child psychologist, while mentoring young children in England, having already established several athletic centers. He is also an inspirational speaker, traveling throughout England and the USA, sharing about his "Plan," how he made it to the top, and also sharing about his life as a gay man in the NBA. He is also a spokesperson for the Human Rights Campaign (HRC), mentoring other gender confused boys and girls. If such a man truly understood the real facts about SSA, what a powerful force he would be to help future generations heal and fulfill their true gender identity. Oprah promoted John on her show, and now John promotes gay rights. (I am grateful to John's publisher for giving me permission to use his quotes liberally.)

PROFOUND FATHER WOUND

John was born in Boston and, at four years old his family moved to Manchester, England to escape his abusive father.

"I should have been overcome with fear about my disgraced father's threats to hunt us down and make us disappear, the fear of losing a comfortably middle-class existence for a new life in faraway land..." (6). "My father, it turned out, became emotionally abusive to his wife" (9). *John's dad left a pile of unpaid bills for his wife to pay. He then returned to his native country of Nigeria. When he returned to the USA,* "Mum made it clear he was no longer part of our family" (9). "As his menacing behavior and his veiled contempt escalated, Mum decided it was time to flee to Manchester" (9).

"My father had sent Granddad a letter threatening to kidnap us and spirit us away to Nigeria, never to be seen again. We knew it was no idle threat, because he did show up now and again, and Mum would sequester us at a friend's place while he stayed in the UK" (11). "When Dad came to the UK, Mum would somehow learn of his whereabouts. We would be driven to the safe house of one of Mum's friends. Our nights away were scary because we knew Mum would be confronting our dad. When Dad finally stopped showing up, I was

116

nearly 10. Only then were we allowed to take our bikes around the block, temporarily out of Mum's watchful eye" (11).

John lived with his Mum, two sisters, grandmother and cruel grandfather; there was no healthy male role model in John's childhood. Significantly, as an adult, when his father died, John had no desire to attend the funeral.

PERSISTENTLY ABUSIVE GRANDFATHER

Besides having a threatening, abandoning father, John's grandfather was also abusive and critical. The lack of a warm and encouraging male figure in John's life created a vacuous hole in his soul. This male mentoring wound and lack of salient paternal love helped to lay the groundwork for John's future SSA.

"Granddad cast a shadow of fear over us. We weren't a bad lot, but he had a knack for making us feel like the worst kids in the world when Grandma wasn't around to keep him in check. As a male role model, something my childhood lacked, he left a lot to be desired. Perhaps his attitude helped me better understand the kids whom I would eventually mentor. Without the warmth from Mum and Grandma to temper Harold's coldness, I might have ended up as furious as he was. Coupled with the bullying I experienced at school and a father who threatened to kidnap us, I understand the reason for my utter disdain for sadistic coaches" (254).

OVER ATTACHMENT TO MOTHER

John's Mum became a medical doctor in Scotland. There she met her future husband Jon Amaechi who was from Nigeria. They traveled to Nigeria to assist others during the Biafran War. Next they moved to Boston and married. John's mother worked at Mass General Hospital and his dad started a manufacturing business. John was born on November 26, 1970. Muriel was born one year later and Uki a year after that. In Manchester, John's Mum worked day and night to support her three children. Eventually she became a partner in a surgical practice. As you read John's words, his role model was his "Mum," as there was no man to show him the ways of men.

"I knew Mum would never allow me and my younger sisters, Muriel and Uki, to come to harm. Through sheer force of will, she surrounded us with a comforting blanket of security" (6). "Mum is the person who was my role model...From her I learned perseverance despite great odds, courage in the face of danger, and stoicism against evil" (7). "Mum tried to protect us from the ugliness of those early days by maintaining a steely silence, so there's much her kids don't know (7). "It was inspiring just watching her take on the world, and the determination she demonstrated rubbed off. Her children have never been afraid of setting goals and letting nothing stop us in the pursuit of them" (12). "What I most hoped to emulate was Mum's bedside manner, her ability to serve as an emotional as well as a medical caretaker, to soothe the hurt, no matter how dire...I still swell with pride when someone stops me on the street in England—not to recognize me as the former NBA player, but to regale me with glowing stories about how Mum touched their lives" (12).

Mum was John's hero, caretaker, protector and mentor. His father was, in his and his mother's eyes, a failure, abusive, and a threat to the family. This was a sensitive boy deeply connected to his mother and completely cut off from and fearful of his role models of masculinity, his dad and grandfather. Robert Bly, in his book Iron John, *details how a boy cannot grow into manhood without the active participation of healthy male figures.* "A mother's protection, no matter how well intentioned, will not do as a substitute for the father's protection" *(Robert Bly, Iron John, Vintage Books, New York, 1990, 67). Bly also speaks about the phenomenon in which a boy is protected by his mother, and thereby learns to feel as a woman, losing his own sense of gender strength and connection to the masculine.* "Jung said something disturbing about this complication. He said that when the son is introduced primarily by the mother to feeling, he will learn the female attitude toward masculinity and take a female view of his own father and of his own masculinity" *(Bly, 24)*. *Furthermore he states,* "If the son learns feeling primarily from the mother, then he will probably see his own masculinity from the feminine point of view as well" *(Bly, 25)*. *As loving and protective as John's Mum was, it disrupted his psychosexual development as a male.*

HYPERSENSTIVE TEMPERAMENT / BODY-IMAGE WOUNDS / MALE PEER WOUNDING

John hated his body. Being a hypersensitive boy, he was unable to stand up to the bullies and set them straight. John's childhood lacked a protective, salient dad or positive male role model to show him the ways of men. No boy can become a man without the investment of positive male role models. Robert Moore states, "If you're a young man and you're not being admired by an older man, you're being hurt." *There was no father around to help strengthen and affirm John's masculinity.*

"By age 10, near the end of primary school, I already stood a head above my classmates at nearly six feet tall. In fact, I was taller than many of my teachers…Not only was I tall; I was brown-skinned and increasingly round…I stood out not so much like a sore thumb but a fat one" (13). "Especially in gym. Donning my first uniform— bright red shorts—belly protruding, was an exercise in humiliation, worse even than Granddad's signature haircut. Team photos were posted on the public notice board, enshrining my shame for the entire school" (14).

John experienced humiliation in his swim class for being overweight. One classmate yelled, "He's supposed to be able to hold his breath: he's a whale!" "It was one of those moments when you swear you can feel a part of yourself die inside. I'd been christened a monster forever. I dunked my head to avoid the rising ridicule. Whenever I showed up for mandatory swim, I'd be greeted with similar name-calling. And it wasn't just one bully. It seemed everyone joined in the fun. All I could do was force out a pretend laugh, but deep down I had to admit the words cut…The experience in the swim class had lasting psychological ramifications. For my entire adolescence I wouldn't get near a public pool without covering my entire body the instant I emerged from the water. Even today I'm rarely spotted anywhere near a body of water." (15). "At any rate, my self-consciousness about my body made me want to avoid sports of any kind" (16).

"I despised exertion of any kind. I hated to sweat. The more strenuous the exercise, the more I loathed it. Even long walks sent me around the bend. To this day, I've never understood those who enjoy the supposed 'high' of intense workouts. To me it is pointless pain and suffering. I've experienced plenty of endorphin surges after an intense workout, but I must say I've had better highs from a cup of Earl Grey tea. Instead, I came up with a far superior activity to pass the time: sitting in a chair reading and drinking enough delicious tea to fill a swimming pool" (17).

John retreated into the world of books. One reason was to avoid social criticism and seek solace in the world of make-believe, magic, and fantasy. No one could hurt him there. You can see the parallel in John's life with that of Melissa, who sought refuge in movies and music, and Greg, escaping the trauma of his life through diving.

"I read and reread every volume in the Hardy Boys series. It never bothered me that every story was identical, save for the setting…It's no surprise my taste ran to the escapist. There were no social pressures or demands, no put-downs directed at me, and it was always others who felt the sting of hurtful words. Like a lot of kids, I identified with outcasts who took on great magical powers to overcome their evil tormentors…The massive amount of time I spent with my nose buried in books helps explain why I had few friends" (17). "Mum threw me a 10th birthday party. Only one kid showed up" (18).

Books and food became substitutes for healthy male friendships, paternal love and affection. There is a book entitled, When Food is Love. *The author explains that many people use food as a substitute for real love in their lives. John used his studies and food to fill those vacuous spaces in his soul.*

"Where athletics failed me, academics made me. I may have been physically loathsome, but with enough reading I figured at least I could be more clever than everyone else. It was my last hope to be exceptional at something, anything, to become an intellectual super-hero" (21).

John studied for tests night and day and still didn't make the top grades he expected. "Fat and dumb. Over and over, I berated myself before bursting into tears" (21). "Along with books, food was my greatest diversion. On the way to Stockport Grammar School, I'd stop at the sweet shop and fill my pockets with Bon Bons, Pear Droops, Cola Bottles, Gummy Bears, Twix, and Kit Kats. Not surprisingly, I ballooned further. The bigger I got, the more I needed my candy therapy. My candy stash did have one advantage: I would offer sweets to kids I hoped to befriend as a sort of bribe. It worked. My 11th birthday party was packed with kids of all sorts" (18).

John's words ring with the same frequency as those of Greg Louganis. Self-deprecation, self-loathing, and low self-esteem were common experiences of both boys. Because neither Greg nor John bonded with their primary role model of masculinity and other buddies at school, they also rejected their own masculine bodies, a common experience of men with SSA.

"Public showering was and is not high on my list of favorite activities. I preferred to head to my next period, sweat pouring off my clothing and onto the classroom floor, to the humiliation of undressing in public" (24). "What I enjoyed was not so much the sport of it [basketball], but the sense of accomplishment and the accolades, which came from every direction with even the slightest hint of improvement" (28). "As a teenager with low self-esteem, basketball had given me a life, but it had also denied me one" (158).

Until John started to play basketball, he lacked any sense of self-worth. He detested his body, disliked sports, and felt different from the other boys. Name-calling was part of his social life at school. Detached from his father and grandfather, detached from the other guys at school, he was also disconnected from his own body and sense of masculinity. This, in my opinion, is what led to confusion about his sexuality and the development of SSA through adolescence.

CONFUSION ABOUT HIS SEXUALITY AND GENDER IDENTITY

"The Plan" John refers to below was what he created with his Mum in order to maintain his integrity while pursuing his goal of being a professional basketball player. He first noticed attractions to the other boys in the high school shower room. Now in college, he began to experiment sexually. He kissed a volleyball team player in the men's locker room at Penn State.

"For days I could still taste the salty sweetness of his tongue, which seemed to have an almost chemical charge when it touched mine. I kept returning so these encounters must have done something for me, fulfilling a nascent longing to be touched, recognized, deemed attractive. They were some confusing combination of fervent, sordid, disquieting, and thrilling all at the same time. That they were not part of The Plan—in fact, they were contrary to it, and that made them even more alluring" (111).

"The pro locker room was the most flamboyant place I'd ever been this side of a swanky club full of martini-drinking gay men. The guys flaunted their perfect bodies. They bragged of their sexual exploits. They checked out each other's cocks. They primped in front of the mirror, applying cologne and hair gel by the bucketful. Some guys just lacked self-consciousness. Others clearly liked to show off. I can't blame them: If I had three percent body fat, I'd probably flaunt it too. They tried on each other's $10,000 suits and shoes, admired each other's diamond studded rings and necklaces. It was an intense kind of camaraderie that to them felt completely natural, but was a little too close for my comfort. I stood in the corner in baggy clothing or wrapped in an oversized towel, dreading having to reveal my body on the walk to the showers. As I surveyed the room, I couldn't help chuckling to myself: And I'm the gay one. Hah" (140).

These comments reveal a significant gender wounding in John's psyche and soul. Men learn to be men by hanging out with the guys. In healthy child development, first a boy bonds with his Dad, or a positive male role model. Next, in the homo-social stage of bonding—between the ages of five to twelve or thirteen—boys bond with other boys. From this, he obtains a healthy sense of his own gender prowess, being one of the guys, a man among men. John missed all of this, revealed by his perception about men joking around, checking each other out, and showing off their strong bodies. All this is viewed through the lens of one who is ashamed of his body, insecure about his masculinity, and sees men from a feminine perspective. Being comfortable about his masculinity and his body is not part of John's experience. Because he was not taught to understand the true meaning of his SSA, John eventually "came out" to his close friends and family, and began to engage in sexual relationships with other active SSA men.

CONCLUSION

When John began to play basketball at 17 years old, he finally experienced healthy male mentoring in the form of basketball coaches. At last some wonderful men devoted their time and attention to him. But unfortunately, the emotional damage from his childhood was already lodged in his soul. And then the cultural paradigm finished the job: "You are born gay and that's that." As with Greg Louganis and Melissa Etheridge, John used his talent to gain love and acceptance, which, nonetheless, didn't heal his broken heart. He had already constructed an emotional barrier, not wanting to be hurt once again by men. After puberty, those legitimate needs for male bonding and connection became sexualized. Until his childhood wounds are grieved and reconciled, no amount of homosexual relations will heal the broken and needy child within John.

As you can see from John's own words, he is a very bright, caring and sensitive man. If he had been given the correct information, the outcome would have been entirely different. Still today, if John would endeavor healing his past wounds by dealing with the initial causes of his SSA, he would be able to fulfill his true gender identity and naturally come into the fullness of his innate heterosexuality.

John entered the NBA: from the Cleveland Cavaliers, to pro teams in Greece, Italy, England, France, back to the NBA with Orlando Magic, Utah Jazz, Houston Rockets, and finally the New York Knicks (although he never played for them). He made the best of each situation. During those years, he mentored over twenty young teenage boys, and became the legal guardian for two of them—giving to them all that he himself never experienced. It breaks my heart that John, and so many others like him, would be living a different and more fulfilling life today if they had been taught the truth about SSA and experienced healthy love from heterosexual men.

Following are some suggestions for healing that would be helpful for John and other men who grapple with similar issues:

1. *John needs male mentors to help break through his defensive detachment— the walls of protection around his heart that he constructed as a young boy to keep from being hurt by his dad and grandfather. John is comfortable in two roles: (1) mentoring boys, and (2) engaging in homosexual relations. Both keep him "safe," but miss the mark to heal the wounded child within.*

   John desperately needed healthy male mentors in his formative years of life. Without a father, and constantly enduring criticism by his grandfather, John never internalized his own sense of masculinity. By joining with someone of the same gender through homosexual relations, his psyche is attempting to fulfill unattained paternal and fraternal love. Dr. Elizabeth Moberly describes this as a "reparative" drive, whereby the individual seeks to bond with men because of unattained love in childhood. In this way he is attempting to incorporate that which is lacking within him, mainly a deficit of masculinity. Sex can never heal those primal needs for love and gender identity.

2. *If an uncle or male friends of the family had stepped up to the plate in John's youth, spent time with him, and showed him the ways of men, this most likely would have prevented John from developing SSA.*

   If you know a young boy who is surrounded by women and has no healthy masculine role model, either stand in the gap for that young boy, or if you are in a position to talk to his mother, perhaps you might suggest someone to her who can serve as a male mentor for her son. Boys need men to initiate them into the world of masculinity. Mothers cannot do this.

3. *Today, if healthy men would befriend John, love him, and put their arms around him, displaying healthy male affection, eventually his anger and pain would arise. Underneath that anger is a hurting little boy. If you know a man who experiences SSA, embrace his anger, allow him to express his pain, and in so doing, his life will be changed forever.*

   The natural process of healing is to grieve. Part of that grief may manifest itself in anger, confusion, rage, frustration, fear, or pain. Be there with the man you are mentoring and listen—you don't need to provide answers. Just be there with him as he releases years of heartaches and pain. Through this process, he will learn to experience love from healthy men who care without any demand for sex, without any demand for performance. What a new experience of love this will be for him, helping to restore his broken heart.

Rosie O'Donnell

I believe that Rosie experiences same-sex attraction, like many other women, due to a combination of factors:

> *1 – Hypersensitive temperament*
> *2 – Insufficient mother-daughter bonding / abandonment*
> *3 – Strained father-daughter relationship*
> *4 – Body-image wounds*
> *5 – Sexual abuse*

I admire Rosie O'Donnell. I read her autobiography, Finding Me (Warner Books, New York, 2002), *as well as an interview she and her former partner Kelly did for* The Advocate. *Rosie is bright, talented, sensitive, amusing, caring, articulate, and brave. Her heart of compassion is matched by her down-to-earth demeanor. Ms. O'Donnell is a busy woman juggling family life, sponsoring and working with an adoption agency, championing and speaking out for homosexual rights, making movies and hosting television and radio shows. After separating from her former partner Kelly in 2009, Rosie became involved with another woman.*

Ms. O'Donnell's autobiography details many of the causes of her SSA. By quoting several passages from her book, I will identify how Rosie is another classic study of why someone might experience SSA.

She was the middle of five children growing up in an Irish Catholic home in New York. Her mother died of breast cancer in 1973, when Rosie was just 11 years old. She and her mother have the same name: Roseann. To her friends, she is known as Ro.

Throughout her autobiography, she shares about her involvement with Stacie, who she believed to be a frightened, wounded and pregnant 14-year-old girl who was raped by her pastor. Against the advice of family and friends, Rosie spent many days, nights, and months trying to "save" her. This is a classic co-dependent scenario, trying harder than the other person to get them well. Rosie helps others, but hasn't been able to resolve her own issues. In the end, Rosie found out that Stacie's pregnancy was a "hoax," and in fact Stacie was a deeply traumatized woman named Melissa who experienced dissociative identity disorder (multiple personalities) and created alternate egos to survive a horrific past. Rosie's account of her relationship with Stacie reveals her own fragile state of being.

I have the deepest respect for Ms. O'Donnell for exposing her frailties. It takes a lot of guts and courage to show such vulnerability. With the aim of understanding what might have caused her SSA, I would now like to construct a portrait of Roseann O'Donnell by using her own words. Thanks to her publisher for granting permission to use her many quotes. I will offer suggestions why she developed SSA. I do this in humility and in consideration that Rosie, like all of us, is a wounded soul looking for love and understanding. (Thanks again to her publisher for permission to use these quotes.)

HYPERSENSITIVE TEMPERAMENT

Rosie worked with expectant mothers in her New Jersey nonprofit adoption agency. Many sexual orientation therapists have observed that those who experience SSA are highly sensitive men and women, responding to circumstances with a heightened sense of emotional awareness and attunement to others' feelings and needs. The shadow or unconscious side of this gift is that most often the individual is not attentive or aware of his or her own needs. Then they seek solace through others, or in the arms of someone else, as their way of saying, "Please take care of me." This is the voice of the child within.

"I know stuff. Stuff I shouldn't. It scares some people. Not me. It started when I was little, before I knew what they were, these ethereal moments where I am given information from some unknown place inside me" (13). "I think I have OCD or ADD or some other three-initial ditty. Whatever it is, it is exhausting" (15). "I can't stand the pain in their voices, the tenderness in their hearts, their struggling souls. Also, I become over involved. To put it bluntly, I have no boundaries. Zero, nada, zippo—none" (5).

INSUFFICIENT MOTHER-DAUGHTER BONDING / ABANDONMENT

Family rule in the O'Donnell house: Don't share your thoughts, feelings or needs (as you may remember, this is the same unspoken code in the alcoholic or high stress family). Rosie was unable to grieve the loss of her Mom. She still has a hole in her soul, longing to experience and obtain her mother's love. This is one contributing factor that may lead to the development of SSA, seeking maternal bonding with another woman, the "reparative" drive. After puberty, this emotional need for bonding becomes eroticized or sexualized. The world then mistakenly says, "You're gay," or "You're lesbian." More accurately, within Rosie is a little girl longing for her mother's love. If you have heard many of Rosie's interviews, she frequently shares about the deep loss of her mother.

"I did not go to my mother's funeral. I went to her wake. It was quite a scene…I saw my stiff sleeping mommy and realized, right then, that she wasn't going to wake up. Then I cried. I cried very hard…On the day I got my driver's license, I went to visit my mother's grave for the first time…I feel I never really got to say a full good-bye. Sometimes I think that may be why I'm still saying good-bye, today. It's like I'm somehow stuck. Mom, Mom. You could just call out forever" (29). "After my mother died, the house and just about everything else fell into total disrepair. It was always dark inside. Life itself was smeared a dull gray. It smelled of dust and stale urine. To me, it smelled of death" (19). "She died. She remains a mystery to me" (23). "There was an awkward silence. Never speak the truth, that's the rule. See her die before your eyes, but say nothing" (26).

STRAINED FATHER-DAUGHTER RELATIONSHIP

In her book, Rosie recalls being estranged from her dad while growing up. He was unable to allow his daughter to express her deeper feelings and support her growth. He was also overwhelmed raising five children alone. Rosie has a negative view of intimacy with men based upon the

relationship with her dad, as well as being sexually abused. There is glar-
ingly very little Rosie shares about her relationship with men, only a
brief mention of abuse but little else. The omission speaks volumes…most
likely, she has much fear of men, but as you see in her appearance, she
dresses and acts more masculine herself…identifying with the perpetrator
to maintain control and power.

"When I was twenty-nine, I fell in love with a man who was sweet and funny and kinder than any man I had ever known. Tall, blond, and handsome, with a stunning smile, we spoke about getting married, which was both thrilling and repulsive. He didn't care what size my body was and no matter how hard he tried to convince me of that, I never believed him. As he and I got closer, I got bigger. For every pound I gained, I took one step backward, using flesh for padding. I bubble-wrapped my heart…I am difficult to love, and I know it. I never learned the unconditional part, so trust evades me. Add sex and I fall apart, eventually retreating back into the swamp" (73). "I knew nothing of boys, and what I knew of men was no enticement to boy-raising" (157).

BODY-IMAGE WOUNDS

Rosie experiences gender detachment, remaining at odds with her body
and femininity. This establishes a pattern to seek self-acceptance by join-
ing with someone of the same gender…in essence, trying to love herself
through another woman, trying to obtain a sense of femininity she never
adequately internalized while growing up. She is typical of most SSA
men and women in that she doesn't like her body. When children fail
to sufficiently emotionally attach to the same-gender parent, and/or
same-gender peers, they generally reject their own sense of femininity or
masculinity. This leads to gender confusion. Rosie, characteristic of many
women who experience SSA, does not like her feminine body.

"Being a girl was horrible and gross. It was the end of the world as I knew it. First I found a lone strand of hair under my arm, and now this [*referring to her menstruation cycle*]. I prayed it was all some sick joke mothers were forced to tell their daughters" (8). "I hate my body. I always have. I hate to admit this fact, but it is just that: a fact. I do not look in mirrors, I try never to be naked. If I could have sex with my clothes on I would. I am the dieting queen, but, along with all the other four billion diet queens in this country, I never stick with the program" (71). "Fat is a protector; anyone can tell you that. I didn't like being 'thin.' I felt like people could come too close" (72).

SEXUAL ABUSE

Many men and women who experience SSA have been sexually abused. I would estimate that half of my SSA clients over the past thirty-five years were sexually abused. Many scientific studies have been conducted, with their results showing that a high percentage of those who experience SSA were sexually abused as children. One potential effect of male sexual abuse upon a woman is her fear of intimacy with men, not wanting to be placed in such a vulnerable position again. Turning to someone of the same gender feels safer and comforting. Rosie is also drawn to "save" other female abuse survivors in an unconscious attempt to heal herself (projective identification). However, this never works.

"I was an abused kid. This is something I have chosen not to dwell on in my public life…So, yes, I had been abused, although the details are not important. What is important is that I had, supposedly, dealt with the fallout in therapy. How naïve I was. Abuse is an ongoing saga for everyone who has lived through it (hence my relationship with Stacie). It may start and stop in real time, but in mind-time it goes on forever" (75). "Why was I drawn to Stacie? Oh, a million reasons, one of which was this: a reliving. A sense of shared pain. Talking to her, I felt this pain, my pain, all over again. And although it's hard to admit, I like how it felt. Electric current, real. It made me feel alive, raw, and sad. I am a swamp person, and so was Stacie" (75). "Maybe it's also an abuse thing. When your boundaries have been violated, you just plain and simple stop seeing the space between people, so people's pain becomes your pain and you have to stop it. At the same time, though, codependency is also a distancing ploy; you're so busy trying to save the world out there you forget about the people close to you, and then, last of all, or first of all, you forget about yourself, that you might be the one worth saving" (78).

As Rosie stated, she has a need to "save" others, yet an inability to take care of herself:

"Show me your wounds, and wait for me to come save you. I will…That's me, 'the queen of nice.'…My giving is impulsive, driven by a demon who also happens to have a huge heart. The contradiction exhausts and embarrasses me" (38, 40). "Stacie had many sides, shifts, and splits in her, as I had in me" (51). "As a superhero, I am sworn to serve. I have no choice really. This need to save people is so strange, because it comes from such a warped place inside me: On the one hand, I think I'm powerful enough to really make a difference; it's sheer disgusting narcissism. On the other hand, I feel so powerless, so much like the people I am trying to help, that I blur the line between me and them…And then there was Stacie herself. Stacie, whoever she was, had become a friend and a reflection, a conduit to the pieces of my own past, pieces I was aware of but had not resolved" (123). "I realized that no amount of therapy, giving away of money, or involvement with other wounded travelers would take away my own damage. I knew I had avoided fully experiencing my own past by living in other people's" (129). "The realizations I came to, through this relationship [*with Stacie*], were at once subtle and profound: Saving the world is a lofty goal and an impossible feat. Swimming in others' pain only delays the journey through your own" (208).

Stacie represents Rosie's own wounded, unhealed inner child whom she is unable to embrace directly. Rosie is emotionally stuck, unable to resolve her childhood trauma, thereby reliving it through others. She works to save others (codependent behavior), at her own expense, disconnected from her wounds and needs. Trapped in a life of same-sex relationships and solving other people's problems, Ms. O'Donnell is unable to access and resolve her own core issues. If Rosie would get in touch with her own inner child, work through a program to heal that child within and experience intimacy with women in healthy, non-sexual relationships, she would heal and fulfill her own sense of womanhood and femininity. Then—naturally—same-sex attractions would dissipate as she becomes comfortable in her own skin.

CONCLUSION

In my opinion, Ms. O'Donnell experiences same-sex attractions, like many other women, due to a combination of factors—hypersensitive nature, gender identity confusion, body image wounds, insufficient mother-daughter bonding, distance from father, and sexual abuse. I propose that if Rosie would work through each one of these issues in her life, experience healthy, non-sexual intimacy with women, and heal with healthy men, then she would ultimately resolve her SSA and experience a sense of inner peace, self-worth, and opposite-sex attractions.

Following are suggestions for healing that will help Rosie and women with similar backgrounds:

1. *The direction of Rosie's life would have been changed if, at the time of her mother's death, her father had been better supported by family and friends, and Rosie had been taken care of by a warm, nurturing mother figure.*

    Sexual abuse is devastating to all children. Rosie needed help as a child to deal with all her confused feelings and thoughts after the abuse. As she mentioned, the way of her family was non-communication of their personal feelings and thoughts. After experiencing any form of sexual abuse, make sure your child, family member or friend gets professional help as soon as possible. Those experiences will not disappear with time. As mentioned, time does not heal all wounds; in fact it only buries them deeper.

    Make sure your family is a safe place for children to express themselves, whatever they are going through, whatever they are thinking and feeling. Listen. Be Mr. & Mrs. KYMS = Keep Your Mouth Shut, and just listen. If Rosie had been able to release her sorrow over her mom's loss and be comforted by loving family members and friends, she wouldn't be stuck in a perpetual state of frozen grief today.

2. *Women who experience SSA need healthy heterosexual women. Most SSA women are looking for healthy maternal and sisterly love in the arms of other women. As we've seen again and again, sexual relationships will obstruct the very thing they seek—to be tenderly embraced and to feel safe, satisfying the need of the child within.*

Kevin Jennings

"I become 'Mamma's boy,'" which is, of course, the worst thing any self-respecting Southern male child can be. I can't remember a time when that wasn't my name. So I guess there was never a time when I felt like I was a normal boy" (*Mama's Boy, Preacher's Son*, Kevin Jennings, Beacon Press, Boston, MA, 2006, p. xii).

Kevin Jennings was the former Assistant Deputy Secretary of Safe and Drug Free Schools, U.S. Department of Education in the Obama administration. In his autobiography, we witness another typical profile of how a hypersensitive boy developed SSA.

As I read Kevin's autobiography, I cried as I learned about his childhood. What a sad life he lived without his father, caretaking his mother, taunted and teased by his older brothers, and incessantly mocked by the boys at school and in the neighborhood. Kevin, another very sensitive soul, was stripped of his pride and dignity over and over again. "Trailer trash" is how he felt about himself. A brilliant boy who went on to become a Harvard graduate, and worked for the U.S. Department of Education, Kevin still carries the many wounds from his past, which I believe led him to experience SSA. (I will summarize most of Kevin's life experiences to honor the request of his publisher.)

What I believe to be the causes of Kevin Jennings's SSA are as follows:

> *1 – Emotionally detached from his father, his role model of masculinity*
>
> *2 – Over-attached to his mother, identifying more with her feminine nature*
>
> *3 – Constant abuse from his older brothers, further disconnecting Kevin from masculine identification*
>
> *4 – Continuous mockery by school and neighborhood boys, more reinforcement for male dis-identification*
>
> *5 – Negative religious messages regarding SSA; constant judgment causing increased shame and guilt for his feelings*
>
> *6 – Lack of protection from male teachers and school administrators, which increased his masculine wounding*
>
> *7 – Hypersensitive temperament, a beautiful characteristic given by God, became a curse because of the unsympathetic environment in which he lived*

FATHER WOUND

Kevin's dad was an angry man and his "spankings were painful, always featuring his black belt" (50). *As a pastor, he preached* "hell and damnation." *Kevin feared his dad, who had a very judgmental nature. His father preached in the South, and southerners didn't like his* "Yankee accent," *as well as his habit of* "sleeping with the deacon's wives" (6). *He lost many positions because of these facts. According to Kevin, the two things his dad cared most about were God and sports, while Kevin was into reading and academics.*

When Kevin was eight, his father was also employed as a construction worker to supplement the family income. They lived in Lewisville, NC. On Kevin's eighth birthday, his dad asked him where he wanted to go and Kevin said the "Y" *to swim. His father, only forty-seven years old, dove into the pool, had a heart attack and died hours later! His mom proceeded to have a nervous breakdown and Kevin was left alone with all his thoughts and feelings. Kevin was led to believe that he was responsible for his father's death. His brothers would tell him so over and over again.*

At the funeral service, his mother fainted and Kevin began crying. His brother Mike barked, "Don't cry. Be a man. Don't be a faggot" (p. 19). *Kevin stopped crying and learned that being a man meant never showing his feelings, even at his father's funeral.* "Any male who deviated from those standards had a name. That name was faggot. That would be me" (p. 19). *He lived in constant fear of reprisal, while name calling and teasing throughout his childhood was the norm. Kevin learned from a young age to repress his grief for his father's death, and to suppress all his feelings. He was consumed with guilt and shame, believing that he "killed" his father.*

MOTHER WOUND

Kevin was over-attached to his mother on the one hand, and fearful of her on the other, as she often beat him. From an early age, he also became caretaker of her needs. At three-and-a-half years old, Kevin had whooping cough and went into the hospital in North Carolina. The family was extremely poor, had no insurance, and therefore they waited too long to seek medical help. He was placed in an oxygen tent with needles stuck throughout his body. It was an extremely painful time for Kevin. His mother was there throughout the ordeal as a constant source of love and support. However, Kevin stated, "I'm not supposed to be here at all. As Mom would tell me repeatedly throughout my childhood. I was not a wanted child" (p. x). *Kevin felt the pain and burden of not being wanted while seeing his mother struggle to take care of him and his four siblings.*

Kevin's Mom was from a poor Appalachian family in Tennessee. She only completed the sixth grade because she was forced to quit school in order to help support her family. Her alcoholic father slapped his wife and kids around, and tried to sexually abuse her and her sisters. Being extremely poor, they often had no place to sleep, and at times would spend nights in abandoned churches. They had no running water or electricity throughout her childhood. His mother picked cotton as a child, did many chores and took care of her siblings. Kevin's mother "hated" her father for these and other reasons. Kevin would hear about this throughout his own childhood. The message was clear: men are mean, men are bad. This message came across to sensitive and impressionable young Kevin as, "Don't be like them, don't be a boy/man, because men are mean and bad and treat women poorly." This kind of accusation emasculates a boy, causing him to put up a defensive wall around his heart towards his own role models of masculinity, his father, brothers, and other boys at school. It also caused him to identify with the feminine, his Mom, and to dis-identify with the masculine, his dad and other men/boys. This created a "double-bind" in Kevin's heart and mind—I can't be a real boy or man because that would further hurt my mom.

After Kevin's Dad died, the family lived on food stamps. His Mother, a proud woman, was humiliated. Kevin had to eat the free lunches pro-vided by the school and felt embarrassed. He was constantly teased by the other kids because of this. "If I said I was hungry, Mom would remind me of how she would wake up crying from hunger as a child, and that her mom would cry too, because often she had no extra food to feed her" (p.35).

Following his father's death, Kevin's Mom pawned her wedding and engagement rings to survive before she got a job working at McDonalds, where she continued to work for most of Kevin's childhood. From the time Kevin was in sixth grade, everyone else had left home, and it was just Kevin and his mother. They lived in a small trailer.

Kevin's Mom gave him a passion for history and learning. He learned about his Confederate ancestors. He would escape his "drab and depress-ing" life by studying history and sharing with his Mom about their background. Even though they were so poor, she bought him the entire set of Encyclopedia World Books, *which Kevin consumed, reading every volume. Now that his father had passed and his siblings were gone, Kevin became the main focus of his mother's life. He learned to converse with her in an adult-like manner, growing up too fast—a parentified child.*

Kevin devoured books, they were his best friends. From the fourth grade, Kevin was bored by books for his age group and started reading adult books; he preferred non-fiction to novels. His mother was extremely bright, and had been ahead of her classmates in school, but had been forced to quit school after the sixth grade by her dad. She was self-educated, read a lot and watched TV to stay informed, but her lack of schooling was always a source of shame for her. Therefore, she fiercely supported Kevin's thirst for knowledge.

Like Greg, Melissa, John, and Rosie, Kevin used his gifts (intellectual prowess) to obtain attention and affection, but of course this was just more performance-based behavior for Kevin, the caretaker, Kevin the brilliant student, Kevin the little boy who took care of his hurting and lonely mother.

Yet even as hard as he tried to do everything perfectly, Kevin's mother went wild when she spanked him, which would last from a few seconds to ten minutes. She sometimes used belts and very hard kitchen utensils to spank him. Kevin feared her hitting him more than his father because he never knew how long she would hit him. This demonstrates Kevin's love-hate relationship with his mother. It also increased his desire to take care of her needs, or identify with the perpetrator, because if she was happy, he wouldn't get hit.

SIBLING WOUNDS

Kevin had one older sister and three older brothers. Carol, the eldest child, was seventeen years older than Kevin. She received little attention from her father because she wasn't into sports or religion. She rebelled to garner attention. Alan, the eldest son, was the kindest to Kevin, but he left when Kevin was quite young. Mike and Paul terrorized Kevin through most of his childhood. He feared their anger and being hit. Kevin lived in constant fear. Name calling and teasing was also the norm.

Again, because Kevin asked his father to go to the Y on his eighth birthday, his brothers thought he was to blame for his father's death. "This wasn't a conclusion I came to on my own. No, my older brothers told me explicitly that it was my fault that Dad was dead" (p. 41). *Kevin's mom was easily upset and his brothers suggested that he might kill her too!* "If I upset my mom—easy to do, as Dad's death and my childhood illness made her more and more jumpy, and an inexplicable absence of more than two minutes would often throw her into a paroxysm of hysteria—my brothers pulled me aside and whispered, 'What are you trying to do, kill your mother like you killed your father?'" (p. 42).

Kevin's brothers used him as a whipping boy, taking out their hurt and pain on him. They also used guilt: besides blaming him for his father's death, they also shamed him into believing that he might kill his mother as well. No child should have to live with such false beliefs. This demoralized Kevin from a very young age. No one was there to defend him. Today, Kevin is the defender of young children throughout the USA.

HYPERSENSITIVE TEMPERAMENT

Kevin experienced a tormented childhood and a hypersensitive temperament that made his life experiences all the more punishing. He did not have the internal strength to fight back, therefore he internalized all the negative messages from his family and peers. Kevin always felt shameful about: (1) his same-sex attraction, (2) thinking he was not wanted, (3) believing that he killed his father, (4) imagining that he might kill his mother, (5) being non-athletic, and (6) being a "geek" because he loved learning.

His father tried and failed to get him on a football team with his brothers when he was underage (Kevin was just six, and the starting age was eight). Still Kevin blamed himself since his father couldn't be wrong; he experienced further rejection and self-condemnation. Kevin's sensitive nature was neither honored nor understood by his family members, relatives, or peers. If you read Kevin's autobiography, you can easily observe the similarities between his sensitive temperament and that of Greg, Melissa, John, and Rosie.

MALE PEER WOUNDING

Name calling—"faggot," "queer," "sissy," "teacher's pet," "nerd"—was almost a daily occurrence throughout Kevin's childhood and adolescence. Being non-athletic and the last one picked for teams in gym class, also contributed to feeling left out. Kevin was terrorized on the bus trips to and from school, traumatized by boys after getting off the bus, and teased and mocked during gym class. Meanwhile, by the age of eight, Kevin had lived in seven or more homes! Being the new kid at school is very difficult for any child and was more so for Kevin, being so sensitive. He was also singled out because he lived in trailer parks, and the other kids ridiculed him for this as well.

"Mom and Dad's spankings, and my brother's bullying, would leave their scars in the form of a clear lesson: when people get angry, they hit you. I developed a lifelong, nearly paralyzing fear of angry people, so much so that I would do anything to avoid getting others angry—anything, no matter how damaging it was to me" (pgs. 52-53). *In the sixth grade, after getting off the school bus, a trailer park neighbor made him sit on the curb until he and the other kids were out of sight. Kevin took it, just sat there, not wanting to upset anyone. The kids called him "faggot" and other demeaning words. This experience was endemic of so many other horrific times Kevin endured throughout his early childhood.*

Kevin developed an immense fear of going to school, which became more and more overwhelming for him during childhood. Kevin gained weight in middle school to avoid dealing with his fears and the incessant daily mocking. One of his brothers called him "Baloney Boy." In gym class, they played "smear the queer" when Kevin got the football, so he experienced verbal and physical "smearing" regularly. He was mocked in the locker room for being overweight. Sound familiar? It's the same story of Greg and John. All of this must have led to body-image wounds, which are typical of so many SSA boys and men.

MALE TEACHER WOUNDING

Nearly all male authority figures had a negative impact on Kevin. Abandoned by his disapproving father, mocked by his older brothers and school classmates, he also felt rejected by his teachers. It wasn't safe for Kevin to become a man. He learned this from his mother, and he experienced it with his dad, brothers, classmates and male teachers.

Not only did the boys tease Kevin in gym class, he was also taunted by Mr. Cultrou, his middle school gym teacher. When Cultrou saw Kevin looking at another boy in gym class, he screamed out in front of every-one, "Stop looking at his legs" *(p. 58). Kevin froze while the entire class stared at him. From that time on, the other kids took Mr. Cultrou's taunting as license to increase their harassment of Kevin.*

Kevin went to the school guidance counselor for help but the man did nothing—simply nothing. No one stood up for Kevin. This pained young boy would later found GLSEN (Gay Lesbian Straight Education Network, as referred to in Chapter One) and become the Safe School Czar for the U.S. Dept. of Education. No wonder Kevin has gone to all this effort to keep other LGBTQ+ kids safe. However, his caring and thoughtful efforts are terribly misguided because he does not understand the truth about SSA.

RELIGIOUS WOUNDS

Kevin's father preached "hell and damnation" *in the* "Southern Baptist Church tradition." *His son was led to believe that homosexuality was the worst* "sin," *and experienced constant guilt and shame because of his SSA. In his mind, he was wicked and evil because he could not control his homosexual thoughts. His* "God" *was punishing and mean, like his pastor-father. There was no hope for him or his salvation, even though he accepted Christ. Kevin lived in constant shame and terror of a punitive*

God, as he lived in fear of his father, brothers, and boys at school and in the neighborhood.

Kevin's father preached in churches, revivals, and crusades. The family's lives revolved around the church, listening to the elder Jennings' "angry sermons." At six years old, Kevin told his father that he accepted Jesus, but his dad responded by saying that Kevin was too young yet to give his life to Christ. Kevin felt unacceptable yet again, assuming that he couldn't even be "saved" by Christ. Something was fundamentally wrong with him. He believed that he was going to hell.

"My dad and our Father (in heaven) had merged together. Right after Dad's funeral, Mom told me that when people die, they go to heaven, where they look down upon you and know your every thought and every action" (p. 40). *Kevin believed that his father was watching as he masturbated, and knew every thought in his mind. This filled him with a great sense of "shame" and "horror."* "My internal policeman would remind me every day: You are bad. You are bad. You are bad. You are bad. So bad you killed your father and want to kill your mother" (p. 42).

Kevin eventually rejected God altogether, because he had prayed for years for his SSA desires to be removed and they only intensified. He had experienced too much shame and guilt throughout his childhood. Now, he had to rid himself of this uncaring, judgmental god. The guilt and shame were too much for such a sensitive, young boy to contain, so he rejected God and his faith.

It is also important to realize how detrimental the concept of "pray away the gay" truly is. Of course God can remove those desires, but he doesn't because they are connected to a broken heart in need of healing and love. I also prayed for 25 years for God to remove my SSA. Finally, I realized that I had been praying the wrong prayer. When I began to pray correctly, "God, please show me the meaning behind my same-sex attractions," the many causes were revealed. Then, step-by-step, I began to experience real healing and lasting change. God always listens. We just need to ask the right questions.

CONCLUSION

After graduating from Harvard and becoming a high school history teacher, Kevin learned about a junior high school student, Robbie, who shot himself in the head after experiencing years of taunting and teasing because of his SSA. "I found myself wanting to find every Robbie in the country and tell him it would be okay, to hang on, that school was the worst part and it would be alright when you got out and could make your own path in life. I started thinking that I needed to view every lesbian, gay, bisexual, and transgender child as if they were my children and fight for them as ferociously as parents like Leslie [Robbie's mother] had fought for theirs" (224). *Kevin has become the voice of the voiceless; however, he has not healed his own wounds as he fights for others (similar to Rosie's journey).*

Kevin was born on May 8, 1963. If you see a photo of Kevin today, or catch him on TV, you would think that you are looking at a much older man. His appearance is saddening. From "trailer trash," to Harvard, to history teacher, to the U.S. Department of Education, this brilliant and sensitive man is hurting, and hurting others by propagating false claims about homosexuality. Kevin's heart is in the right place, but he lacks a true understanding of what drives his and others' SSA.

Here are suggestions that could help Kevin, and men like him, find healing:

1. *I wish a trustworthy man would hold Kevin in his arms and tell him, "You are wonderful just as you are. You are not responsible for your father's death. You were not responsible to take care of your mom (as a child). Your brother's cruel words only reflected their own pain, projected onto you. The kids in the neighborhood and at school were repeating what they had experienced from their own parents. It was not about you Kevin, it was always about them." "You are wonderful. You are strong. You are masculine. It's good to be a boy. It's good to have feelings. It's good*

to express your feelings and share your thoughts with others."
"When anyone speaks about you in a negative way, just look into
their eyes, see their own pain, and know that is has nothing to
do with you." "You, Kevin, are God's precious son, made in His
image. You have so many wonderful unique talents and gifts.
You will bring much healing and light into the world." "Kevin,
you are loved just for who you are. You don't need to do anything
to deserve or earn love. You are loved just for who you are." "God
loves you Kevin, homosexual feelings and all."

As a former SSA boy and man, I understand Kevin
from the inside out. As an adult, married man with a wife and
three children, two of which are men, I want to express love to
Kevin, show him how fantastic he is, and assure him that his
SSA is merely a representation and accumulation of so many of
the unresolved wounds from his past and legitimate needs for
healthy masculine love. "Kevin, sex with another man will never
bring you what you truly need," I'd like to tell him. "You need
to taste the love of healthy heterosexual men, men who can bless
you, men who will have your back, men who will listen to your
pain and let you grieve in their arms."

FINAL CONCLUSION

I hope the stories that you have read in this chapter will inspire you
to reach out to the Kevins, Rosies, Johns, Melissas and Gregs of this
world. They are hungrily looking for love. If they'd had healthy male
or female mentors while growing up, the outcome would have been
entirely different. If we could only begin to set love in order, eventually there would be no children who experience SSA and other
wounds of the heart. There are always predictable causes for SSA—
and those causes can be avoided or, if necessary, reversed.

It took me over one year to write this chapter—reading their
autobiographies and capturing the meaning of their wounds. I cried

many tears while writing these evaluations. I see them as my brothers and sisters, and I love each one of them. There is no reason why men and women who experience SSA must suffer like this. We have answers and solutions. We need to spread the truth in love to save lives. The next two chapters will describe how we can rightly love those who experience SSA. But first, Susan's story.

Susan's Story

I am including this particular story because it is representative of those who receive help from religious-mediated ministries and/or religious supported change efforts. Since the early 1970s, the mental health profession abdicated responsibility for the scientific investigation about the causes of SSA and successful therapies for those who experience unwanted homosexual feelings. As a result, many para-church ministries have sprung up around the USA and throughout the world (see a list of Organizations at the back of the book). They filled a vacuum that the mental health profession created.

Radical transformation is possible. I lived 18 years of my life as a lesbian with absolutely no desire to change. Now that I have been set free, I am experiencing the most wholesome and unconditional love of God, and will never turn back!

I was born in 1963, to a 19-year-old mother and a 21-year-old father who had lost their first child, my older brother, to complications during childbirth less than a year earlier. My parents both came from homes where their same-gender parent died when they were very young. I am the oldest of three biological children of my parents and one adopted sibling. I was brought up in the Catholic Church, and early in my life, I developed a love for God and even dreamed of becoming a nun.

I was extremely insecure as a little girl and did not make friends easily. I never really connected with kids my own age, and my best friends were always older than me. I matured quickly, and beginning at the age of 9, I took on the role of babysitter for my younger siblings as well as the 50 foster children (infants) that my family took in over a period of 7 years. I felt like an adult, even as a child.

In junior high school I began dating a boy who was several years older than I. He lived quite a distance away, so he would come and spend the weekends at my house whenever possible. During this time, my mother started to go with us to the movies or bowling alley nearly every time we went out. She never really dated as a teen because she was raising her two younger brothers. She married my father at the age of 16 to get away from her alcoholic father and her dysfunctional family.

When I was 15, my boyfriend and I were away at a church camp, and there he tried to have sex with me. When I returned home, I talked to my mother about it, and her reply was that I should give him what he wanted. To make matters much worse, soon I found the two of them together in her bed! This sent me spiraling into a deep depression. I rejected God and completely turned my back on him, denying that he even existed. I struggled for the next several years with deep depression and attempts at suicide. I graduated from high school, my parents divorced, and I went to college in another part of the state. There, I experienced being sexually assaulted by three different older men and further rejected any notion that God could exist. I thought what I knew as a child was just a lie and a fairytale—there was no God. I actively rejected the existence of God, telling people who believed that they were weak and deceived.

I built an impenetrable stone wall around my heart and started dressing like a man, making my appearance completely undesirable to men. I befriended my college roommate, and she showed me non-sexual love. We started sleeping together, and she would just hold me, and I felt safe. Soon I became extremely jealous when she started dating a man and he moved into our house. I had to endure the pain of hearing them together in the next room, and I was alone once again. I began to struggle with the thought that I was truly a homosexual. I even sought out counseling, and the therapist said that I was a homosexual and should just embrace it.

I entered the Army at the age of 24, and there met a woman who introduced me to homosexuality. At first I felt safe and loved. However, she was involved with another woman as well, and my relationship with her was an emotional rollercoaster. During that time, I was also seduced by two different married men who wanted to have sex with me, and I gave in to them because I was looking for love and struggling with who I was sexually. I ended up completely embracing homosexuality and began to live as a closeted homosexual in the military. My first homosexual lover eventually left me after a rocky 6-year relationship, and I spiraled back into deep depression. I truly felt like I would die.

In 1993 I began dating a woman who went to church, and one day she invited me to join her. I said that there was no God and that I hadn't crossed the threshold of a church since I was 15. She looked me straight in the eyes and said, "Jesus wants you back." At that moment, the Lord began to break down the barriers in my heart and I began traveling the road back to him. I personally experienced what the Bible says in Ezekiel 36:26-27: "I will give you a new heart and put a new spirit within you; I will take the heart of stone out of your flesh and give you a heart of flesh. I will put My Spirit within you and cause you to walk in My statutes, and you will keep My judgments and do them."

I joined the Metropolitan Community Church (MCC), a homosexual church. I became indoctrinated in their beliefs that God made me homosexual and that he was pleased with my lifestyle, and I became very involved in the church. Over time, I discovered that the woman who brought me back to church was an alcoholic, and I suffered both sexual and emotional abuse in that six-year relationship. In January 2000, I left her behind and moved to the Washington, D.C., area and sought out another MCC church. I entered into another homosexual relationship in April 2000, and the two of us were warmly accepted by the gay community where we lived. In 2001 we traveled to Vermont and entered into a civil union. We began to build our life together. We bought property and built our dream home, co-mingling everything we owned.

I became unsatisfied with the MCC churches I had found, so I began to seek out other types of churches. My partner and I found a church that we loved the first time we attended service. I was shocked and disappointed to see the word "Baptist" on the sign out front as we left the church that first day. I just knew that "they" would not accept us there. However, we continued to go to that church and were warmly greeted by everyone. We were determined that over time we would bring change to the church and eventually they would openly accept gays as we showed them that our love for each other was pure.

When this church began a church-wide Bible study, we opened our home to host a small group study (which was facilitated by a leader in the church), and at the end of that study the church was having a celebration service and invited anyone who wanted to be baptized to sign up. We requested baptism, and were both called into the assistant pastor's office, where he told us he didn't know if he could baptize us since we were living in sin (we had been "ratted out" by the church leader who facilitated the small group in our home). After a long discussion we both told him that we would walk away from our lifestyle if that is what God told us to do, so he agreed to baptize us. That was November 23, 2003.

Over the next 2 years, I became more and more involved in the church. I volunteered as one of the production managers for Sunday morning services, and became heavily involved in the women's ministry. I also developed a love for the Word of God, which is where the REAL transformation in my life began to occur. My partner and I started to read the Bible together every day, and when we would come across passages about homosexuality, she would question me and I would immediately respond with the "real truth" I had learned at MCC about what the scriptures meant. I firmly believed what I had been taught. All the time, unknown to us, the women's ministry leaders at the church were just loving us where we were and praying fervently for our deliverance.

In the fall of 2005, I approached the women's ministry leader and said that my partner and I wanted to "come clean" with the women in our ministry (believing that nobody in the group knew we were gay). She suggested that we meet with the pastor to discuss this before talking to the women's group, so we began a series of meetings with him. The pastor asked me why I labeled myself as homosexual. I answered that I was born that way and felt I needed to tell him who I was because my lifestyle didn't conform to what the church teaches. He said he just saw me as a child of God. They confronted our beliefs in a gentle and loving way, never backing down from their convictions, but gently showing us what the scriptures said about the way we were living. Over time, the Lord convicted us through his Word—the Truth.

We decided to follow the Lord at all costs. We were determined to live out what the Bible says in Luke 9:23: "Then He (Jesus) said to them all, if anyone desires to come after Me, let him deny himself, and take up his cross daily, and follow Me." On January 1, 2006, we publicly confessed to the women's group at church that we were turning away from our homosexual lifestyle and following Jesus. We began by moving into separate bedrooms in our house, and eventually, my partner moved out completely. This was an extremely painful time, but we were determined to do what was right. It felt like a physical death, with the loss of physical touch and the struggle to redefine myself. I didn't know who I was anymore, because I had identified myself as a lesbian for 18 years, and at that time had actually convinced myself that I had always been homosexual. I thank God for the healthy heterosexual women who surrounded me with love as I suffered through this transition.

As I drew closer to Christ, he began to reveal to me the things that had occurred in my past that led me to embrace a lesbian lifestyle, and God began to heal those deep wounds in me. I also grieved the loss of what my life could have been if I had married and had children, realizing now that I may never marry and have a family of my own.

I cannot begin to tell you how much God has blessed me since I have completely turned away from denying his existence and leaving the homosexual life for a total of 24 years now! God did such an incredible thing in me—I feel as if he actually transformed my DNA. Please be encouraged by my story, whether you are struggling with same-sex attraction, or you are a family member or friend of someone who is, because change is possible! [Today Susan leads a major ministry in her church helping those who experience SSA and their loved ones.]

CONCLUSION

Have you identified some of the causes of Susan's SSA? Here are at least some of them:

1. Susan was detached from and wounded by her mother, her gender role-model of femininity. Susan's mother was an adult child of an alcoholic (ACOA). As we've seen, in the alcoholic family system, experiencing one's feelings, thoughts and desires is not an option. Having missed her youth, she leaned on Susan to help raise her siblings and foster children. Her mom also sought a sexual relationship with Susan's boyfriend. This deeply traumatized Susan. She felt betrayed by her mother, which led to her rejecting God. (Children often reject their parents' belief in God when they reject their parents.)

2. Hypersensitive temperament: Susan was highly attuned to her mother's feelings and that of others. She was a natural caretaker, but this gift was used to win the love and affection of others. Susan became more and more detached from her deeper self.

3. She experienced low-self worth and had no close friends among her own peers. Susan only related to older kids, typical behavior of what is commonly called the "parentified" child. The parentified child knows too much, too soon, and thereby takes on the characteristics and behaviors of an adult.

4. Susan was sexually abused and used by men. She began to dress like a man so as not be perceived as sexually desirable or

attractive to men. The unconscious thinking goes something like this: "Women are weak so I'll act like a man. I will also camouflage my femininity so men will not find me attractive" Of course these thoughts may be completely unconscious. This may have contributed to her gender dis-identification as a woman.

5. Socialization into the homosexual myth. Susan was groomed into lesbianism by women who showered her with attention and affection. She sought her mother's love in the arms of these women.

SUGGESTIONS

Here are some ways family members and friends may help a woman like Susan:

1. It is apparent that Susan lacked a healthy relationship with both her mother and father. She never mentioned the participation of her dad in her life. Not only was there wounding with her mother, but her father also left a hole in her heart, not providing her with a healthy image of men.

   In Susan's healing, wonderful women in her church provided the first source of healthy feminine love. This is a beautiful example of how heterosexual women may naturally help SSA women heal and fulfill their innate heterosexual potential.

2. Susan was sexually used by men, as she sought to heal the father wound, and finally turned to women for safety and love. She still needs healthy men to demonstrate positive masculine love and concern. As the parentified child, Susan is comfortable taking care of others. It is more threatening to allow others to care for her.

   Just as wonderful women began to love and mentor Susan, so men also need to shower her with healthy male affection, restoring the misuse and abuse of the men who hurt her. Naturally, she may be defensive at first by any attempt of men to display healthy concern and affection. However, in time, with persistent effort, the walls will come down and the love will come in, just as it did with her healthy female mentors.

3. Speak loving words into the lives of those who have either experienced or experience SSA: "I love and accept you just as you are." "You are beautiful and feminine." "I love you Susan." Because she was hurt by her mom, missing a masculine father, and sexually abused by men, she needs lots of positive affirmation from both men and women.

Chapter Four

Words that Hurt / Words that Heal: Language to Restore Wounded Souls

> We've learned about the potential causes of SSA. How punishing to someone who is already in pain to hear words like "faggot," "queer," "sissy," "dyke," "pansy." It's like we are kicking someone who is already down on the ground and bleeding.

In this chapter, I will present terminology coined by homosexual activists. Many of these words or terms were created through years of research, spending hundreds of thousands of dollars to construct language to help us accept and love people who experience SSA. It bears repeating that SSA is an emotionally-based condition. We need to promote love in the *truth*, accepting people who experience SSA and at the same time helping them to reclaim their true heterosexual potential.

Let's look at the strategy behind the activists' terminology and try to introduce new and more helpful language. You will discover how "tolerance, diversity, and equality" must be extended to *both sides* of this issue, to (1) active homosexuals, and (2) those who experience unwanted SSA and/or former homosexuals, all coexisting together in mutual respect. To further this goal, I will present their terminology and offer suggestions to increase healing and reconciliation:

- No more hate speech, only loving words
- No more gay, start using SSA
- No more sexual orientation, only heterosexuality
- No more same-sex marriage, only marriage
- No more homophobia or anti-gay, only words and actions that heal
- No more hate crimes, only loving deeds
- No more LGBTQ+ or questioning youth, only hurting people
- No more "Love the sinner and hate the sin," only standing with our SSA family members, friends, colleagues, co-workers, and neighbors
- No more "once gay always gay," only "no one is born with SSA" and "change *is* possible."

Words can hurt. Words can heal. We often, unknowingly, wound each other daily with ill-chosen words. Generally we don't think about the meaning of what we are saying or their effect upon those who listen. Let us look at the language and terminology commonly used regarding homosexuals and homosexuality, again, language which was carefully crafted by members of the homosexual movement to promote acceptance.

Most of their terminology (e.g., gay, lesbian, bisexual, transgender, non-binary, queer, homophobia, anti-gay, same-sex marriage, sexual orientation, domestic partners, internalized homophobia) is intended to both normalize homosexual behavior as well as create sympathy in our hearts towards those who live a homosexual life. All people who experience SSA have incurred social prejudice—every one of them. They had to survive and feel some semblance of self-respect and self-worth. Part of this process took place through the creation of language intended to elevate them to equal status. The desired outcome was to experience a sense of dignity amidst bigotry.

For centuries, those who experienced SSA were called derogatory terms. In places of worship, homosexuality was spoken about as the "worst sin" and an "abomination," most often without providing hope or any realistic solution. Having never chosen to have homosexual feelings, they felt trapped and condemned, through no fault of their own.

Gay strategists coined new language to normalize homosexuality. They strategically took the emphasis off of homosexual *behavior*—anal sex, oral sex, mutual masturbation, fisting—and placed it solely on homosexual *identity*: "We are born gay; God made us this way; gay is not what we do, it's who we are." Think about the strategy put forth in *After the Ball* by Kirk and Madsen (1989): *Whoever frames the debate wins the debate.*

No more hate speech, only loving words

Words can hurt. Words can heal. In terms of homosexuality, some words that kill the human spirit are "faggot," "dyke," "sissy," "homo," "pansy," "femme," and so on. If you have spoken any of these or other derogatory terms toward anyone you might have suspected as experiencing SSA, then I recommend you do the following things:

1 – Cease and desist
2 – Apologize and ask forgiveness
3 – Use healing words from now on

We either build each other up or tear each other down. We reap what we sow. Once again, every person who experiences SSA has felt too much guilt and shame. It is time we embrace all SSA people in word and deed, whether they choose to live an openly homosexual life or seek change. All are deserving of our love and respect.

Healing words:

"I love you just the way you are."

"I support and stand with you."

"I think you're terrific."

"You're a fantastic man."

"You're a wonderful woman."

"Please help me to understand your same-sex attractions."

"Please forgive me for using negative words in the past. How did it make you feel when I said such things?"

No more gay, start using SSA

Regarding the use of the "gay" word, this is a delicate balance. I suggest that you stop using the gay word when referring to people who experience SSA. The real definition of "gay" is happy. The term was usurped by homosexual activists to describe a person who experiences SSA. Believe me, many who experience SSA are *not* happy. The "gay" word also denotes someone who has accepted their homosexual identity. It has become a socio-political statement. When we say, "You're gay," instead of, "You experience SSA," it locks someone into a false identity, as no one is essentially born with SSA. There is no such thing as a homosexual (a noun). There are only people who experience same-sex attraction (an adjective describing one's thoughts, feelings, and/or desires) and/or participate in homosexual behaviors. It is important that we separate the person from his or her thoughts, feelings, and/or desires. We may do so by no longer using "gay," but instead describing him or her as someone who experiences SSA.

Additionally, many gay identified individuals now like to be called "queer." Queer has become the new gay. Transgender is another evolving fashion of the day. Terms are changing daily. On Facebook there are over 70 terms a person may choose to describe their gender identity and sexual preference. *Sexual plurality is the new fashion.*

Hollywood stars, political figures, TV personalities, and famous writers are coming out as LGBTQ+. Innocent youth are being persuaded to follow their example.

> Every man and woman who experiences SSA is a latent heterosexual stuck in early stages of psycho-sexual development. When they heal those early wounds, and fulfill their legitimate needs for love in healthy, same-gender, non-sexual relationships, they will experience the fullness of their own sexuality and opposite sex attractions may ensue.

By calling someone gay, lesbian, bisexual, transgender, queer, etc., we are reinforcing their woundedness. We do so by keeping them sheltered in a false identity, and thereby prohibiting them from maturation into their true manhood or true womanhood. Start removing the word and concept of "gay" from your vocabulary regarding those who experience SSA. Let us call forth all persons with SSA into their true heterosexual potential.

> Healing words:
> "I understand that you experience same-sex attraction."
> "I understand that you are attracted to the same-gender."
> "Oh, so you experience same-sex attraction, or SSA?"
> "I respect and accept you just as you are."
> (I will explain in a moment why this last phrase is most important.)

I am fully aware that most gay identified men and women are not aware of the term SSA. Most people under the age of thirty have been co-opted into the "born gay and cannot change" myth. The purpose of introducing new language is twofold: (1) to reframe the homosexual issue—no one is essentially born this way and change is possible,

157

and (2) to bring the homosexual issue back into the realm of psychology and spirituality. This is not a human rights or social justice issue if we truly love all men and women who experience SSA or question their sense of gender identity, i.e., transgender, non-binary, etc.

No more sexual orientation, only heterosexuality

The term "sexual orientation" was created by members of the Gay Rights Movement to gain public acceptance, while subtly indoctrinating us into believing that people are born with SSA. If it's a "sexual orientation," the implicit meaning is that someone has been this way from birth. You may remember the term "sexual preference" which was introduced into our culture previous to the coining of the phrase "sexual orientation." Homosexual activists realized that using the word "preference" implied choice. Therefore, they quickly discarded that term and replaced it with "sexual orientation," which implies that one's sexuality is not chosen but fixed and cannot be changed. I suggest that we stop using this false paradigm of "sexual orientation." It is inaccurate and misleading.

By the way, don't let homosexual activists try to convince you that homosexual behavior is natural in the animal kingdom. This is a gross distortion of situational behavior that takes place within certain species. "Preferential homosexuality is not found naturally in any infrahuman mammalian species. Masculine/feminine differences and heterosexual preferences are quite consistent up through the phylogenetic scale" (W. Gadpaille, "Cross-Species and Cross-Cultural Contributions to Understanding Homosexual Activity," *Archives of General Psychiatry* 37, 1980, pgs. 349-356). "Although homosexual behavior can indeed be found in the animal kingdom, it is not the rule, and when observed, is unusual" (Phelan, J. E. (1998), "Deviated copulation among animals," *Journal of Evolutionary Psychology*, *19*(1-2), 41-50).

Healing words:

"We are all heterosexually designed. Men and women fit perfectly together."

"I understand that you are attracted to people of the same sex, and I believe that we are all heterosexually designed."

"Changing from Same-Sex Attracted to Opposite-Sex Attracted is possible."

No more same-sex marriage, only marriage

The term "same-sex marriage" sounds like a fluffy new flavor ready to grace your palette. It is meant to normalize homosexual behavior—anal sex between two men, oral sex between two men or two women, mutual masturbation between those of the same gender. As we have already learned, people who engage in homosexual activity are like little kids in adolescent or adult bodies, looking for lost or unattained love. It is a cruel and unreasonable action for us to endorse something that will ultimately betray the very essence of these men and women, prohibiting them from achieving the fullness of their innate heterosexual potential.

One who follows the path of least resistance says, "OK, let them do what they want in the privacy of their own homes. It has nothing to do with me." But alas, it may have everything to do with you if you unknowingly marry such a person, have a child, relative or close friend who experiences same-sex attraction. Then, it hits home! How about future generations? Do you want your kids and grandkids to be solicited into homosexuality?

We need to stand with and for people who experience SSA, and love them to life. Please do not inadvertently endorse a behavior that would hurt a family member or friend, or enroll future generations into a false way of living. I recommend that we not use the term "same-sex marriage." Remember the story of *The Emperor's New Clothes*…speak the truth.

Healing words:

"I am neither homophobic nor anti-gay. I love all people who experience SSA."

"I do not believe that homosexual behavior will help an individual fulfill her or his potential."

"I believe no one is essentially born with same-sex attraction, and therefore they may change and fulfill their heterosexual identity."

"I believe in natural law, that marriage is meant to be between a man and a woman."

I fully appreciate the fact that there are many homosexual couples who want the same rights as heterosexual couples. I am not commenting on the civil rights issue. Our path now is to promote true healing for all who experience SSA and be agents of change.

No more homophobia or anti-gay, only words and actions that heal

Homophobia: "Irrational fear of, aversion to, or discrimination against homosexuality or gay people" (Merriam-Webster's Medical Dictionary, 2022).

Phobia: "Exaggerated fear of; intolerance or aversion of" (Merriam-Webster Dictionary, 2022).

Homo: "a gay person—used as a term of abuse and disparagement" (Merriam-Webster Dictionary, 2022).

Anti-gay: "opposed to or hostile toward gay people or gay culture" (Merriam-Webster Dictionary, 2022).

The terms homophobia and anti-gay are grossly misused and misunderstood. Gay activists created these terms to make themselves appear as victims by anyone who does not endorse their homosexual identity and behavior. Brilliant, but wrong. We love those who experience SSA while having a principled disagreement with their homosexual behavior; these two concepts are not mutually exclusive. Disagreeing with their behavior does not make us homophobic, anti-gay, fearful or condemning. One is not homophobic or anti-gay because he doesn't agree with a behavior that he thinks would do harm to the individual. In such a case, there is only a difference of opinion, which needs to be accompanied with love and respect. All people who experience SSA have a choice to act upon their desires or to seek change. *The feelings were not optional, but what they do with them is.*

Healing words:
"I may not agree with your homosexual behavior, *but* I love you just as you are!"
"I love all people who experience same-sex attraction."
"Please do not label me as homophobic or anti-gay just because I do not agree with you. We are all entitled to our own opinions. I respect yours, please respect mine."

There is also the term "internalized homophobia," which is assigned to someone who has internalized negative social or religious attitudes towards their own or someone else's homosexuality. Again, this is a false and confusing term, created to promote a one-sided argument. I may disagree with someone's homosexual behavior and love them at the same time. Do not accept the term "internalized homophobia" if you do not approve of a specific behavior. This is reverse discrimination rearing its ugly head!

Healing words:
"I love you just as you are."
"I may not agree with your behavior, and I love you just as you are!"
"I have a different understanding than you. I respect your opinion, so please respect mine. Let's both practice true tolerance, real diversity, and equality for both sides of this issue!"

No more hate crimes, only loving deeds

We must stand up against those who discriminate against all persons who experience SSA, whether they decide to live a homosexual life or seek change. Words and deeds either kill or uplift the human spirit. *Let us be change agents in the world!* World peace begins with me, my family, and my community. If you see anyone acting violently towards persons who experience SSA, either stop them or contact the police. Defend those who need defending. You could be saving your own child's or friend's life. If you hear someone speaking disparagingly about a person who experiences SSA, kindly correct them.

Healing words:

"It hurts me when you speak about same-sex attracted people in such a way. I have learned that they are not born this way. They do not choose to have same-sex attraction, or SSA. They may change from SSA to opposite-sex attracted. I know of people who came out of homosexuality and are living their heterosexual dreams."

"Excuse me. Please do not use those words around me. I know people with same-sex attraction, and it hurts both them and me when you say such things."

"Would you want people to speak about you in such a way? I am sure you don't mean to hurt anyone, but those kinds of words do. Thank you for understanding."

No more "LGBTQ+" or "questioning youth," only hurting heterosexuals

We have discovered already that LGBTQ+ terminology was created to gain public acceptance for those who experience SSA. Kirk and Madsen's Homosexual Manifesto (*After the Ball*, 1989) set the wheels in motion to increase acceptance but not a real understanding about homosexuality. Now it is time to catch up and set love in order. It is time to speak words that promote real love and truth in the world.

We are straight and late. We need to turn things around, much like the desensitization, jamming and converting strategies we've heard about. Let's stop using terms such as lesbian, gay, bisexual, transgender, queer, questioning and non-binary. When we say the word homosexual, there is a visceral experience in our body letting us know something in incongruent. Sit for a moment, and repeat the word "homosexual" five times. How does it feel? There is almost always cognitive dissonance when we say the word homosexual.

Now say the word "gay" five times? How does that feel? When you say the word gay, there is a pleasing, pleasurable physical and emotional sensation in your body. I know that most of us have been anesthetized by the gay and lesbian terminology (through the process of desensitization). The gay word was chosen to promote the acceptance of homosexual persons. We need to *reframe* the issue in order to help SSA persons heal. Anyone who experiences SSA is not gay, lesbian, bisexual, transgender, queer, etc.; they are all latent heterosexuals.

Are you wondering, what is a "bisexual," or is there really such a thing? The simple answer is, "No." Anyone who experiences attractions for both men and women is stuck in an early stage of psychosexual development. It means that there may have been some degree of bonding with either the same-gender parent and/or same-gender peers, but obviously it was insufficient. The byproduct is SSA. He or she may have also experienced some wounding with members of the opposite sex. There are always reasons locked within the human psyche that explains such a phenomena. Once again, one and one equals two, men and women fit together; two men, or two women simply do not. My personal and professional experiences are that SSA is always a symptom of unresolved issues and unmet, legitimate needs for healthy non-sexual love. If someone is attracted to both genders, they hold some wounding in their mind and heart, and when released, heterosexual desires alone will emerge.

You may wonder, "If someone comes out of homosexuality, will they, like others in recovery, have to struggle throughout their lives with those desires?" It's the wrong question because of an incorrect understanding about SSA. Homosexual feelings are the result of specific unresolved wounds from the past, and unmet legitimate love needs (for healthy male or female bonding). If someone engaged in homosexual behavior and/or viewed homosexual porn from a young age, then neural pathways in their brains were created. Through repeated activities over time, these neural patterns became strengthened. In the healing process—when one grieves, heals past wounds, and fulfills basic love needs in healthy, non-sexual same-gender relationships—those attractions diminish and opposite-sex desires emerge. However, if such an individual is under stress, those old neural patterns may reemerge, as a fall-back, a way to medicate or block emotional pain. This does not mean they will always "struggle" with SSA. It is only past neurological patterns resurfacing, and as I tell all my clients, this is a message from your soul merely attempting to get your attention. Once the individual understands what was troubling him or her, the SSA dissipates, sometimes within seconds.

Another word to avoid is "transgender." Those who believe themselves to have been born the wrong gender harbor profound wounding in their soul. One such gentleman came to our office for help. He looked and acted like a woman, having had hormone injections for several years that increased his breast size. He was contemplating sexual reassignment surgery (removing his penis and building a vagina). He became my teacher. "As a man, no one listened to me or took me serious. As a woman, now I have their attention and people respect me and what I have to say." He felt mistreated and disrespected as a man (having been called every derogatory name from childhood, both at school and in church). Because of his hypersensitive temperament, he didn't have the strength to stand up and push back. He also feared his father and gender-identified with his mother and sisters. He wanted to be like them, while craving the attention and affection of men.

His parents actively participated in his healing process. His dad learned how to love this sensitive young man, accept him for who he was, and spend time together. Other men in the community also came around him, pouring healthy masculine love into his hungry spirit. Many repented for horrible acts of bigotry toward him when he was young. They grieved and healed together. Today, this young man no longer takes hormone injections; he has a beard and once again refers to himself as a man, using his birth name. Change *is* possible!

And here's another term to avoid: "questioning youth," referring to adolescents who might be confused about their sexual identity. Scientific studies show that at least 25% or more of teens question their sexuality because it is a very fragile time of development. With the high rate of divorce and kids growing up in single-parent families, it is understandable that many question their sense of identity and sexuality. Homosexual activists are trying to solicit fragile and confused teens into believing they might be SSA and therefore adopt a homosexual identity.

No more "questioning youth." Let's speak about confused kids who need mentoring and the right kinds of love to help them navigate through their adolescent years successfully. Many adolescents experiment sexually with their same gender friends. This does not mean that they are homosexual or experience SSA. Going into adolescence boys are closer to boys and girls to girls. They often experiment with each other before moving into their full heterosexual identity.

The mantra of the homosexual community is "tolerance, diversity, and equality." I have been a sexual orientation therapist for three and a half decades. I have spoken on university campuses, at scientific symposiums, religious conferences, as well as on hundreds of media interviews. Homosexual activists have attended many of these events or participated in the interviews, screaming at me, speaking with anger and espousing abusive words. One of their tactics is character assassination: criticize the messenger so people will not hear the message.

I am a man of love and compassion. I have never spoken ill of SSA active persons. I lived that life. I would never utter such hurtful words. What I do is share possibilities of change for those interested. I respect the right of self-determination and autonomy for every man, woman, and adolescent—deciding to live a homosexual life, or deciding to change and come out of homosexuality: Life, liberty, and the pursuit of happiness.

Many who demand "tolerance, diversity, and equality" have themselves become the most intolerant and prejudiced individuals. They are critical and condescending toward anyone who does not agree with their viewpoint. Every time I give a presentation or engage in an interview, and face those who mock me or condemn my work, I turn off the volume, look into their eyes, and see a wounded child crying out for love. There he is, hurting and angry, "Please love and accept me." There she is, "Help me, I am in so much pain."

> Healing words:
> "Homosexual persons."
> "People who experience SSA."
> "No one is born with same-sex attraction."
> "I believe in true tolerance, real diversity, and equality for all people."
> "Tolerance swings both ways. Equality and justice for all!"
> "Each man and woman who experiences SSA has a civil and human right to decide if they wish to live a homosexual life or seek change."
> "Are you against an individual's right to choose change? Are you against their right of self-determination? Since when are people denied their right to life, liberty, and the pursuit of happiness?"

There's another phrase I hope you will avoid. I highly suggest *never* speaking to a self-proclaimed homosexual person with the words "I love you, but not your homosexuality (or homosexual behavior)"

This all boils down to "Love the sinner but not the sin." This does not work with this population because they have been indoctrinated into believing, "God made me gay." "God made me a lesbian." "God made me transgender." "I'm born this way and cannot change." This has been the systematic mental programming over the past five decades. To them, homosexuality is not just what they *do*, it is who they *are*, the very essence of their being. Therefore, in this instance, the concept of separating the sin from the sinner *does not work*. We have to understand their viewpoint and love them intelligently.

With this understanding, I suggest saying the following words exactly as written, "I love you just the way you are." These eight magic words commit your unconditional love and regard to the person without any conditions or stipulations. Your family members or friends do *not* need to change in order for you to accept and love them. Don't worry if they misinterpret what you say, assuming that you are endorsing their homosexual behavior. Let them think what they want. If they ask, "Does that mean you accept my homosexual behavior or homosexuality?" Smile and say, "No, and I love and accept *you* just the way you are." Be sure you smile when you say that. This will create cognitive dissonance in their mind because you are now demonstrating unconditional love while disagreeing with their actions. *This is higher love. This is real love.* [While you may think this sounds like deception, in reality it is not. This *is* real love.]

> Healing words:
> "I love you just the way you are."

For four decades we have been inundated through the media, movies, television, schools, politics, Internet and in some instances from various faiths, with the homosexual myth—"born gay and cannot change; once gay always gay." It is time to dismantle this man-made social construct. Kirk and Madsen, and other homosexual strategists, did a fine job in their efforts to stop socialized prejudice. This is a wonderful achievement of the homosexual movement. But somewhere along the line they buried the truth from themselves! We need to dismantle the lies and replace them with real facts about SSA.

Healing words:
"I don't believe that you were born with same-sex attraction. I have learned that people can and do come out of homosexuality. Change *is* possible!"

Conclusion

I strongly recommend that we stop using terminology that was created to promote the acceptance of homosexuality and start using language that uplifts, embraces, and restores these fine and sensitive men and women. In this way, we become part of the solution every time we speak. Be an ambassador of true tolerance, real diversity, and equality for all.

No more hate speech, only words of apology and love. No more "gay," only SSA or same-sex attraction. No more "sexual orientation," only heterosexuality. No more "same-sex marriage," only marriage. No more "homophobia," "anti-gay," or "hate crimes," only words and deeds that demonstrate love and acceptance while fully understanding the meaning behind SSA. No more "LGBTQ+," "queer," or "questioning youth," only people who experience SSA and are latent heterosexuals. No more "Love the sinner and not the sin," only, "I love and accept you just the way you are." No more "Once gay always gay," but instead, "Change *is* possible for those who wish to come out of homosexuality."

Let us reframe the debate. Make a clear distinction between homosexual *behavior* and homosexual *identity*. Every time we use the "gay" word, we reinforce a false concept of homosexuality and imprison people. As Gandhi eloquently stated, "Be the change you wish to see in the world." Sam's story is a wonderful example of change, made possible by a loving and godly mentor.

Sam's Story

This is a beautiful story about the power of mentoring. A wonderful man intervened in Sam's life and dramatically altered his destiny. Enjoy reading about the power of love.

I was either insane, trusting, or being driven by God to talk to Sarge. He was a three-tour Army veteran, complete with a Purple Heart and other medals. I had completed one tour. We were in Virginia. I was going through school, and he was one of the instructors.

I'd gotten to know Sarge because I was being selected to stay on and attend school and become an Army instructor for parachute rigging. I could sew well, and I was a meticulous packer. I was also attracted to other men but had been keeping away from gay bars and sexual association on the advice of a therapist I had been seeing prior to being drafted into the Army. I had been an active homosexual from the age of 14 until I was drafted at 19.

I was on an airplane back to Seattle from San Francisco. I had been there because on my 17th birthday when I told my mom I was gay, she sent me, as a gift, to live with three gay men she knew in San Francisco. I had a great time there ... but on the plane trip back I was seized with the question, "Why am I queer?

I spent time reading Freud, Adler, B.F. Skinner, and others and began to understand some of the issues. This was 1967, so psychologists didn't encourage anyone to experiment and accept the feelings. I met with one therapist who started working with me, but then I was drafted.

The Army was good for me. When asked if I was a homosexual, I said no. And through boot camp, Ranger school, and even in-country, I was following the advice of my therapist. I still had feelings for men from time to time, but the urges seemed under control.

And then there I was, sitting outside a packing shed with this Sergeant, and I started telling him how I felt about men. That I was attracted to them, that I had a dad who ignored me, a stepfather who terrorized me, and an uncle who locked me in a closet, and on and on. Why did I trust him? God knows. But there I was. And when I finished and was getting up to run away, he said,

"Ya know something, Son? Y'all ain't queer. You just need a real daddy."

"Yeah, right," I said.

"No, y'all need someone to show you how to be a man."

"I am a man," I responded.

"Well, ya sort of are. You're part way there. ... Y'all come over for dinner. This ain't no place to talk, all right?"

So I went to dinner at his home. He and his wife said grace. I didn't believe in any god, as my parents were atheists and so I had grown up without a divine influence, albeit a fairly moral one. My father was an objectivist ... Ayn Rand's philosophy.

After dinner he and I sat outside and we started talking. He just pretty much listened without judgment or comment.

"Y'all need to come over here on Saturday and help me."

"Doing what?" I asked.

"I build birdhouses for the church sales, and I need you to cut wood and paint. By the way, ya know there ain't no queer deer, don't ya?"

"What?"

"God didn't make no queer deer. Takes two to make babies."

"OK ..."

"A man needs to know that he's responsible for his family, needs to have a family in order to become more of a man. ... Any of your homosexual friends grownups? You ain't got to answer now. I just want you to think about it. ... See you for dinner on Saturday. Bring your manners with you."

And this started a routine of me coming over for Saturday dinners as well as Friday nights. Sarge used to tell me, "Y'all get them feelings for a man, you come to the house. We'll just talk, and I'll put you to work cutting wood and painting, and we'll have a beer." When I asked why a Southern Baptist had beer in the house, he said, "Well,

Son, I don't hide it from the Lord. I don't get drunk. I like a cold beer now and then, and if I know a fellah's got a problem with his liquor, then I offer him lemonade."

Sarge taught me how to fish and how to make birdhouses. His wife taught me how to make buttermilk biscuits and how to be a man toward women. I was always invited to church socials and to services on Sunday. Sometimes I went, but I was not convinced.

Sarge helped me get my license for parachute rigging and introduced me to skydiving. He took me hunting with other vets and showed me how to whittle a bit. He never told anyone that I was struggling, but he'd ask me how I was doing with my feelings.

"Y'all are gettin' better these days. I seen you lookin' at the cute forklift driver the other day."

"Her name is Susan," I said.

"You think she's pretty?" asked Sarge.

"Beautiful red hair, green eyes, and shapely, too," I reported.

Sarge replied, "You sure you used to like boys? You startin' to sound like a lusty fellow to me!"

"I seem to be thinking about that from time to time," I said.

"Well you know there's a proper time for all that sex, don't you?"

"Yeah, yeah. Mrs. B told me it waits till marriage."

"God says so, too. And though I know you ain't one to talk much about God, I want you to think about Him. I'd like you to know Him personally, too. I got some books for you, cuz I know you're a thinker. ..."

He'd bought some books by Francis Shaeffer and C.S. Lewis for me, and a Bible with lots of ribbons in it marking passages. These were my birthday presents from him and his wife. "You got some reading to do ..."

I put the books away.

I spent almost two years going to see Sarge, building birdhouses, talking, fishing, going out into the woods for one reason or another. We played catch, rough-housed, and went shooting. Basically I found a dad I could love and who loved me. When I left for school, he asked about the books. I promised I'd read them. I did. It would be years later before I became a Christian. But I'd stopped having sexual attractions for other men. I knew Sarge and his wife had prayed many a prayer over me. He used to hug me and kissed me on the cheek on the rare occasion. As far as I know, only he and his wife knew of my struggle. They did what no one had done before: loved me, listened to me, helped me as I struggled, and provided for me a stable home and a steady diet of love. I also learned that a man could do many things like cook, sew, and paint and still be a man of character with leadership qualities.

Sergeant Balderidge died about twenty years ago, and his wife followed shortly thereafter. But he had pictures of me, my wife, and my two children on his piano at home. To him, I was his son.

CONCLUSION

I know more details about Sam's history than those he has related. Here are some of the causes of Sam's SSA:

1. Sam was deeply traumatized by his father and step-father. There was emotional, mental, and physical abuse. Therefore, he never bonded with a healthy male role model before meeting the Sarge.

2. Sam was over-attached to his mother, and thus he had internalized her femininity. As we have learned through the other stories, many SSA boys are close to their moms and more distant from their dads. This precludes them from experiencing their own male gender identity. Instead they over-identify with women and their femininity.

3. Sam was hypersensitive. This temperament led to his feeling different from the other boys at school. As a result, he felt like an outcast, looking in and wanting to belong. Being in the military was actually very healing for him. There, for the first time in his life, he belonged, and he fit in with other guys.

4. After puberty, Sam's legitimate need for male bonding became erotized. Then he engaged in numerous homosexual relationships. However, this never satiated his deeper need for bonding, connection and acceptance by healthy men.

SUGGESTIONS

How family and friends can help a man like Sam:

1. The Sarge demonstrated what I have been sharing throughout the book: Reach out, embrace, listen and love the unloved. Be a father to the fatherless. Be a mother to the motherless. "Restore the years the locusts have eaten" and SSA strugglers will eventually come into the fullness of their true gender identity.

2. Sam lived a homosexual life. It didn't work. Finally, with the help of Sarge, he experienced his own power as a man. When a guy feels his own "guyness," no longer will he need another man to complete him. Opposites attract. If a man feels his own masculinity, then he will be drawn to the opposite, a woman. This occurred in Sam's life.

3. Sam's SSA subsided when he was surrounded by men. If you want to help someone come out of SSA, surround him or her with positive and healthy gender role models. The homosexual community has created many venues for SSA people to gather and feel accepted. It's time for us to do the same, but this time, by demonstrating real love.

Chapter Five

How to Positively Love Our LGBTQ+ Family Members and Friends

Darkness cannot drive out darkness; only light can do that.
Hate cannot drive out hate: only love can do that.

Martin Luther King, Jr.

My friend was drowning. He was sinking fast. I jumped into the lake, put my arm around him, pulled him to the surface, and swam to shore. After performing CPR, he slowly regained consciousness and began to breathe. I saved my friend's life.

So it will be when you put your arms around someone who experiences SSA. You can help save someone's life. Remember the pain Greg Louganis, Melissa Etheridge, John Amaechi, Rosie O'Donnell, and Kevin Jennings experienced while growing up. They were drowning, and no one came to pull them out of the water. Today, they are in a *trance*, indoctrinated into the homosexual myth. We can actively help them—and those like them—heal and fulfill their innate heterosexual potential. *Change is possible.*

This book is a primer, a Homosexuality 101 course, as it contains the basics about SSA: how the homosexual movement gained so much ground in such a short period of time, the hidden meaning behind same-sex attraction, why some celebrities experience SSA, new language to promote healing, and finally practical strategies to love those who experience SSA the right ways and thereby solve the homosexual dilemma.

Many of us were simply ignorant about the facts regarding SSA: no one is essentially born this way, no one simply chooses to have SSA, and change is possible. Perhaps we have even spoken disparaging words about homosexual persons or to an individual who experiences SSA. With greater knowledge come new opportunities to become part of the solution. In this chapter, I will offer simple suggestions and skills to set love in order and heal the brokenhearted:

- Apologize for wrong doing, thinking, and speaking
- Spread the truth about SSA
- Love those with SSA the right ways

Apologize for wrong doing, thinking, and speaking

Instead of condemning, mocking, or blindly endorsing homosexual behavior, we need to understand the situation of those who experience SSA and apologize for any wrongs we might have committed out of ignorance. Please take responsibility for any harsh words or hurtful actions:

Healing words:
  "I am very sorry for what I said [name specific words]."
  "I am sorry for what I did [name specific behavior]."
  "Would you please forgive me?" [After apologizing, ask the following:]
  "How did my words or behavior make you feel?"

After you ask for forgiveness, please be sure to listen to what your SSA friend or loved one has to say. You don't need to have all the answers. All you need is to hear them. Listen to their heart, their pain, their journey. Most of us don't want advice, we just need to be heard and accepted for who we are. That is one of the greatest gifts we can offer to another person. Listen without judgment and accept them just as they are.

Don't be surprised if your SSA family member or friend does not want to open up. They may not feel safe at first, and that's OK. Just apologize without expectation. Let them know that if and when they are ready to share, you will be there for her or him.

Another key to enhance communication is to ask, "How did my words or behavior make you feel?" This is an invitation for the SSA person to reveal his/her heart more deeply. Just listen, be Mr. or Mrs. KYMS: Keep Your Mouth Shut. Just listen. It bears repeating: no answers are required. Be a good listener to what they have experienced. As the Beatles sang, "All you need is love, love. Love is all you need!" This time, you love in full knowledge about the truth of SSA.

Healing words:
"Thank you for what you've said. Again, I apologize for any pain that I have caused you. If you have anything else to share, I am here for you. I love and accept you just the way you are."

Realize that those who have adopted a gay identity believe they were born that way; therefore, do not frame your apology around the causes of their SSA because they do not believe such things… yet! Simply apologize for hurtful words or deeds. That's it, that's all. Dr. Elaine Segal, a psychologist in New York City, wrote a book entitled *Female Homosexuality: Choice Without Volition.* In her book she recounts working with a group of self-proclaimed "lesbians" who had no intention of coming out of homosexuality. However, due to successful therapy with several of these women, one by one, they began to lose their SSA and develop heterosexual attractions.

If the man or woman you are listening to gets angry, that's a good thing. Underneath all psychological anger is hurt and pain. Eventually, after they start running out of steam, the tears may begin to flow. Be patient, allowing her to release years of heartache. Basically, it has nothing to do with you, it's about her pent up emotions—feelings you never knew about. You are providing a safe space for her to blossom and grow.

Spread the truth about SSA

- No one is essentially born with SSA
- No one simply chooses to have SSA
- Change is possible

If anyone repeats a lie long enough and loud enough, over time it is believed to be fact. The homosexual movement has used this strategy, which is known as the Big Lie Theory, to proliferate the homosexual myth—*born gay and cannot change.* If you take a frog and place him in boiling water, he will try do jump out; on the other hand, if you put a frog in cool water, he will happily swim around. Gradually, you begin to turn up the heat, and the frog doesn't notice. Eventually the water reaches boiling point, and the frog dies!

Over the past five decades most of us have been indoctrinated into the big lie theory of homosexuality. We have been boiled alive! The media (radio, newsprint, magazines, Internet), educational system (primary, middle, high schools, colleges and universities), mental health organizations (American Psychiatric and Psychological Associations, American Counseling Association, American Medical and Pediatric Associations, etc.), entertainment industry (television, movies, streaming platforms), political venues, and some religious institutions, all drank the Kool-Aid. We were *desensitized* (like frogs in a constant barrage of homosexual stories), *jammed* (made to feel bad if we had any misgivings about homosexuality or homosexual behavior), and *converted* (celebrities and political figures endorse homosexual persons and their relationships, and therefore so should we).

> Again, Kirk and Madsen stated, "You can forget about trying right up front to persuade folks that homosexuality is a good thing. But if you can get them to think it's just another thing, meriting no more than just a shrug of the shoulders, then your battle for legal and social rights is virtually won" (*After the Ball*, p. 177).

Voila! *Fait accompli*! Wait a minute, not so fast. Time to set the record straight.

Now that you have discovered the *real* facts about SSA, it is time to let the cat out of the proverbial bag—time to come out! Come out, come out, wherever you are. Share the truth about SSA with your family members, friends, at your place of worship, in your schools, at your workplace, and everywhere in your community. Don't expect most folks to say, "Wow, I didn't know that. That's really cool!" You may hear just the opposite, "You're crazy. You're homophobic. You're anti-gay. Everyone knows that people are born gay. There's even a gay gene they discovered. Don't you know anything?"

> Healing words:
> "I learned that people are heterosexually designed, and that no one is essentially born with same-sex attraction or SSA."
> "In fact, changing from SSA to opposite-sex attraction is possible!"
> "I know that many people have successfully come out of homosexuality and are living fulfilled heterosexual lives."

Revolutionary! You can be loving and truthful at the same time, and not be homophobic or anti-gay. This is *loving in the truth*. As I said in the introduction of this book, "Truth without love is blind. Love without truth is deadly." Wherever you are, wherever you go, please spread the truth about SSA with a smile on your face and love in your heart. Thousands of men and women have changed from homosexual to heterosexual. I did it, and as a therapist, I have helped hundreds around the world who experience SSA fulfill their heterosexual destiny.

Wherever you go, whatever you do, set the record straight! I attended my youngest son's soccer and baseball games, and I spoke to the parents while we were cheering our kids on. We got to sharing about this and that, and what we do for living. I always tell them that I am a sexual orientation therapist, helping those who experience unwanted SSA fulfill their heterosexual dreams. "What? Really? Is that possible? I thought they were born gay." That's what almost everybody says, regardless of their religious background or ethnicity. "Really? I thought they're born this way."

No, folks, it's not true.

Instead, when the subject of SSA comes up, say something like this: "Did you know that no one is essentially born with same-sex attraction? There is no conclusive scientific evidence that people are born that way." Some folks will not care, others will challenge you, while still others may be curious and engage in conversation. Set the record straight! Set the record straight! Set the record straight! Use every opportunity to share the truth in love. The pen *is* mightier than the sword. Words are powerful weapons. Ideas bring change and healing to the world. *Speak up, stand up, and let the healing begin.*

Loving those with SSA the right way

> Endorsing homosexual behavior may give some what they want, but it will never give them what they truly need.

We are the solution to this situation. By understanding that men and women who experience SSA are either seeking paternal/maternal and/or brotherly/sisterly love allows us to step up to the plate and stand in the gap, embodying the love of God in a tangible way. Therefore, OSA (Opposite-Sex Attracted) men, please bless SSA men with healthy, masculine love. The same holds true for SSA women. They are seeking maternal and sisterly love. Women, if you are attracted to the opposite sex, please bless SSA women with healthy, feminine love. There has been far too much judgment of SSA men and women. Today there is too much blind acceptance of homosexuality. *It's time to set love straight!*

For too long SSA men and women were despised simply because they experienced homosexual feelings. Now, in the name of diversity and tolerance, many are endorsing homosexual behavior, thinking they are helping to right the wrongs of centuries of unjust persecution. The healthiest position is to love all people with SSA, while at the same time helping them discover their true nature and gender identity.

As you read the stories of transformation, you saw that these men and women were desperately seeking attention, affection, and affirmation *Sex never satisfied their needs because those feelings originated in childhood, and children do not need or want sex.* SSA is always a smoke screen for unresolved wounds from the individual's past, and primal needs for love yet to be fulfilled. Healthy relationships with heterosexual men and women will provide the love and healing they need.

Here are three simple action-steps to help any SSA person fulfill his or her heterosexual potential:

- **Listen**: Learn how to *listen* well. Hear their stories without judgment. Let them share their truth and experience being accepted for who they are. Keep repeating, "Thank you, tell me more."
- **Love**: This is a person who has experienced much rejection and shame throughout his or her life. Be there for him/her. This is the solution to heal SSA: heterosexual men embrace SSA men, and heterosexual women embrace SSA women. *Be God with skin for them.*
- **Last**: Be the last one standing. If they are gay identified or seek change to fulfill their heterosexual dream, they need your time, touch, and talk. Statistically most homosexual relationships do not last because both are seeking what neither one of them have. SSA men are seeking healthy paternal and/or fraternal love, trying to incorporate their lack of gender identity by joining with someone of the same sex. SSA women are doing the same. If homosexual relationships do last, they most often become platonic in nature. *If you continue to love your SSA friend or family member, you will be the last one standing and able to help them heal and fulfill their innate heterosexual potential.*

Listen

Communication is like air for all relationships. Without sharing and listening, relationships wither away and die. Active listening is caring for the other person, showing that you are interested in his well being. Here is a list of effective listening skills; however most imperative is that you have a heart of concern.

Effective Listening Skills:

1. *Eye contact. Look into his eyes as he shares.* This lets him know that you are actually listening and connected to his sharing. It expresses acceptance of the speaker.

2. *Joining:* Join her rather than offering advice or your opinion; see from her viewpoint. Imagine what life is like living in her shoes. You don't needs answers; just "join" with her as she shares about her life.

3. *Observe his body language, tone, and words.* Research shows that more information is communicated through body language and in the tone of one's voice than through actual words. Be attentive to his posture and tone. And remember that your posture is equally important to him. Lean forward as he shares, and have an open facial expression. Do not fold your arms across your chest, as this often demonstrates emotional distancing.

4. *Be quiet and KYMS: Keep Your Mouth Shut!* You don't need to have the answers, just listen as she shares from her heart. Bite your tongue if necessary when you completely disagree. Most of us don't need answers, we just need to be seen, heard, and accepted for who we genuinely are. Remember, be Mr. or Ms. KYMS!

5. *Reflective listening.* This is a skill to reflect back what the speaker has shared. This wonderful skill works in all relationships, with our spouses, children, boss, co-workers, and friends. Practice using this on a regular basis. It helps you deescalate when you feel like attacking the speaker. It also enables you to see life through the other person's eyes. As suggested by Dr. Harville Hendrix, here is a threefold technique to teach the art of reflective listening:

    a. *Paraphrase his sharing (in small increments).* For example, you paraphrase: "You felt offended when I said, 'I don't think that people are born with same-sex attraction.'" Then say, "Is that right?" or "Did I get it right?" If you're wrong, don't worry; he'll correct you. If you left something out, he will tell you. As he continues to share, paraphrase again. Then say, "Is there more?" Listen, and reflect again. Keep paraphrasing, and asking, "Is there more?" When he says, "No, that's it," then summarize the basic contents of what you heard. Finally say, "Is that essentially what you shared?" or "Did I understand you correctly?" If he said you got it all, then proceed to thought empathy.

Don't put your personal thoughts, feelings or inflection when you paraphrase. It's OK to 100% disagree internally. You just need to *join* with him and reflect what you heard. In this way, he feels understood, regarded, and respected.

b. *Thought empathy*: "You make sense to me because …" For example, "It makes sense to me that you do not agree with my belief, because you think that you were born with SSA. Is that correct?" Here you imagine how he *thinks*. You are validating his thoughts. After you finish say, "Is that right?" If he thinks it's wrong, don't worry; he'll correct you. Then paraphrase what he shared and say, "Is that right?" If you got it, move on to feeling empathy.

c. *Feeling empathy*: "Given all that, I imagine that you feel …" For example, "I imagine this makes you feel hurt, offended, and upset? Is that right?" Again, don't worry if you're wrong; he'll correct you. Then repeat what you heard, "Oh, you feel …"

When you paraphrase what he said, make sure to use the same tone as the speaker. If you use a sarcastic tone, this will invalidate everything he shared. Remember, you don't need to agree; just listen. This takes a lot of practice and patience. Keep breathing.

6. Use the magic words: *"Thank you, [person's name], tell me more."* Again, you want to see life from his viewpoint. Get out of the way and say, "Thank you [person's name], tell me more." You will be very surprised how grateful another human being is to be genuinely heard. In the process, your heart will be changed as you come to understand life through their eyes.

7. *Silence.* This is one of the greatest gifts you can give another person. Don't fill the empty moments with words, comments or questions. Just "be" with her in the silent moments. It allows her to know that you are "there" for her, and it gives her the opportunity to go deeper into her mind and heart.

8. *Don't look at your watch when someone is talking to you.* This demonstrates to the speaker that you want him to finish. If you have to look at your watch, only do it when *you* are sharing.

9. *Ask gentle, non-invasive questions*: "What was that like?" "How did that make you feel?" "When did you experience that emotion before in your life?" Don't ask "why" questions, because that brings the speaker into her head. Ask open-ended questions starting with "how," "what" or "when." Of course, do not be confrontational, as this will create a barrier between the speaker and you.

Practice these skills with your spouse, relatives, friends and co-workers. Like physical exercise, it takes time to develop muscles. Practice these listening skills when things are good. Then when your SSA friend or loved one is upset, you will be ready to effectively listen.

Be aware that some men or women who experience SSA, at times, may act like a three or four-year-old, throwing a temper tantrum, demanding that everything go his or her way. Of course, we may all act like this from time to time. This behavior is connected to the wounded child within, basically a lack of bonding and bound-aries—if the child didn't sufficiently bond with his or her parent(s), if the child was indulged and not properly disciplined, if the child was abused, if the child didn't learn how to emotionally self-regulate, these and other unresolved issues may manifest in adult tantrums.

You will need to stand firm, loving and unyielding in the presence of their immature behavior. This is time to truly demonstrate real love for the hurting child who is locked deep within the adolescent or adult. Understand they may lack the ability to emotionally *self-regulate*, and don't know how to express themselves more responsibly. Listen but do not allow him to abuse or attack you, for this will not benefit him or you. "Please do not speak to me in such a manner. It is very hurtful. What do you need right now? How are you feeling?" Then listen, reflect, and continue to hold a space for them to unfold.

A note about sharing the real facts about SSA with LGBTQ+ identified men or women: *Don't do it!*. Really, *don't do it.* Their lives are constructed upon two pillars: (1) "I am born gay," and (2) "I cannot change." If you so kindly and lovingly say to this person, "You know, you weren't born with SSA and you can change." Pow! Sock in the heart! You just pulled the rug out from underneath him or her. Remember the seven stages of coming out. They went through years of confusion about their SSA, years of struggle to numb their conscience, and then, against all odds, it took years to feel comfortable living as a homosexual man or woman. Now you say, "Hey, you weren't born this way and you can change." "Well, thank you and (blank) you!"

If you wish to share the facts about SSA with a LGBTQ+ identified person, first ask yourself these questions: "Am I doing this out of love? Am I willing to be there and listen to what s/he has to say? Am I willing to get involved in this person's life? Am I willing to listen, to love and to last in his life?"

If the answers to your questions are, "Yes," then go for it (prepare your heart, and seek coaching if you need assistance). If not, just give as much as you are able to this person...or ignore everything I just said, and follow your heart!

Love

Love is not only a noun, not just a feeling that we have for another. It is also a verb. It is the actions by which we express care and concern (TLC: Tender Loving Care). Love is demonstrated by our behavior. It shows our acceptance and genuine concern for the other person's happiness. There are many activities that express our love for another:

1. *Spend time with him or her.* In his book, *Five Love Languages,* Dr. Gary Chapman discusses different ways in which we experience love:
   - *Words of affirmation*: verbal compliments, words of encouragement and affection.
   - *Quality time*: spending time together, giving her your undivided attention, quality conversations, quality activities.
   - *Giving and receiving gifts*: giving gifts represent an expression of love, give the gift of your time, make something special for him.
   - *Acts of service*: do something for her that she cannot do for herself, teach her a skill.
   - *Physical touch*: healthy touch communicates care and concern (more about this shortly).

Even if you just spend a few hours per week with this SSA man or woman, it lets him or her know that you care and are thinking about them. Send emails, text messages, call her on the phone just to say "Hi" and ask how she's doing. Random acts of kindness help heal the wounded heart.

> By understanding the causes of someone's SSA, you are better equipped to know exactly what they need to heal their wounds and fulfill unmet love needs, i.e. close relationships with male or female mentors (restoring the parent-child wound), hanging out with heterosexual friends (restoring homo-social wounds), words of affirmation about his or her gender identity (restoring both homo-emotional and homo-social wounding), etc.

2. *Mentoring.* A key ingredient to help all SSA men and women is mentoring. Almost all same-sex attracted men and women missed this important rite of passage into manhood or womanhood through bonding rituals with their father/mother and male/female peers. Some simple ideas for male mentors are taking the guys fishing, camping, athletic games, movies, etc., or accompanying women on shopping trips, participating in their hobbies or going out for coffee. Again, as you learn about their backgrounds and understand the areas of wounding, you will know more specifically which activities will help him or her heal. If he's into the arts, you may want to join him by participating in his interests.

These essential experiences join men together, finally allowing the SSA man to feel a sense of belonging to his own gender. From this inner strength and sense of internalized masculinity, he is then capable of being a man with a woman, attracted to the opposite, something that is mysterious and unlike himself. Of course, this process takes much time, as it took years for him to develop SSA.

SSA women need to be embraced and mentored by heterosexual women. Most of them missed this important rite of passage into womanhood through bonding rituals with their mothers and female peers. Remember the heartaches of Melissa Etheridge, how she never internalized her own sense of femininity because her mother never took the time to teach her, or show her how to be a girl and young woman. We learn about our own sense of gender identity through mentoring during the formative years of childhood and adolescence. If we missed those important stages of development, still, the heart yearns for those legitimate needs to be fulfilled, no matter how old one gets. Therefore, heterosexual women, please spend time with SSA women, mentor them in the ways of women, share with them, and make them feel as though they too belong to your world.

Susan lived a homosexual life for 18 years (earlier, you read her story of transformation). She had several long-term partners, but eventually came out of homosexuality. She was embraced by many heterosexual women in her church, even though she was still living with her female partner. These women surrounded her with beautiful and supportive love and wouldn't let her go. Susan and he partner broke up because it became more and more unsatisfying. Basically, she grew out of SSA as her true femininity was called forth into the world of women. Additionally, her reading the Word of God and learning from her elders transformed her heart and mind.

Healthy bonding helps heal SSA men and women.

My father was unable to demonstrate healthy paternal love, not because he wasn't a good man, not because he didn't love me, just because he hadn't experienced it himself. What I longed for was the same thing that he himself longed for and never experienced...a warm and caring father. Phillip, Peter and Russell, three wonderful, loving, heterosexual men, mentored me back to life. They listened to my pain. They held me through the dark nights of my life. They were there, filling in the gaps of my past. Without their active participation in my life, I would never have healed and perhaps I would have died of an HIV/AIDS related disease, like my former partner did.

It wasn't always easy for them to hear the horrors of my life. I know I put them through their paces. But true men they were, listening, loving, and lasting in my life. Because they were willing to journey with me on this path of healing, I was able to eventually recover my true self and experience the fullness of my masculinity, becoming the powerful man that I was always meant to be.

There are many similar stories from men and women who have come out of SSA and fulfilled their heterosexual potential and dreams. Jeff Conrad, as described in his book, *You Don't Have to be Gay*, mentored a friend who was living an active homosexual life. Through his patience and care, eventually his friend came out of homosexuality. Story after story of loving men and women, standing side-by-side with SSA strugglers, testifies to the fact that loving in the truth will eventually set them free. Listen to more stories of transformation at: http://www.voicesofchange.net.

3. *Speak your truth.* SSA men and women generally feel excluded from the world of their own same gender, like someone on the outside looking in. Please share about your life and your personal struggles. It's a revelation for many SSA people to realize that other men and women struggle with similar issues. Remember, SSA is not really about sex, it's about lack of successful bonding and belonging with one's own gender. The healing of SSA is helping a man fit in with other men, and enabling a SSA woman to fit in with other women.

Let the SSA person know that we OSA folks are just as messed up as they! The causes are so very similar, just the manifestations or symptoms are different. Everyone is dealing with something, as no one had perfect parents, and we are certainly not living in a warm and supportive cultural environment...yet! Please read my latest book, *Healing Humanity: Time, Touch and Talk,* to learn how we may all heal.

Your personal sharing is not to burden the SSA man or woman, but to help them see the commonality among fellow human beings—we are all broken and in process, we all have issues.

As Goethe said, "Treat a man as he is, he will remain so. Treat a man the way he can and ought to be, and he will become as he can and should be."

Speak affirming words into his life:
"You are a strong man."
"You are very masculine."
"I admire and love you."
These are words that will both heal his soul and call him forth into his true masculine identify. Do the same for the SSA woman:
"You are a beautiful woman."
"You are very feminine."
"I admire and love you."

4. *Apologize for wrong doing or speaking if applicable.* It's OK to make mistakes. "To err is human, to forgive is divine." Let him know that you did not understand about his life and suffering before.

Healing words:
"I am truly sorry for all the thoughtless and cruel things I have spoken about you and others who experience same-sex attraction. Would you please forgive me?"
Then listen and paraphrase as you look into his eyes.
You don't need to provide answers. Just demonstrate care and concern.

5. *Say, "I love you."* Many SSA people never heard, "I love you," from their parents or good friends. This need for affirmation and acceptance most often became eroticized during and after puberty. They seek love and acceptance through sexual behavior. It never works.

> Simple words to heal the lonely and broken heart:
> "I love you just as you are."

Repeat these words often, calling them forth into their true gender identity. "I love you just as you are." Again, many SSA men and women never heard these words from their same-gender parent or peers.

6. *Create warm and welcoming homes and places of worship.* My motto is: **This is a battle of love, and whoever loves the most and longest wins.** The prize in this case is the very soul of a precious SSA man or woman. The homosexual community has created many organizations and places for homosexually-identified men and women to hang out, feel safe and accepted. It is our turn now, to turn the tide and create warm and welcoming homes and places of worship where all SSA persons may feel safe, loved, and accepted.

Perhaps you read the book or saw the movie, *The Blind Side*. This is a beautiful example of a family who welcomed in a young man who had no "home," except living on the streets. This courageous act of love saved Michael Ohr's life and put him on the road to success.

- Educate your family members about the truth of SSA.
- Share this book with family and friends.
- Tell them about the stories of change.
- Visit websites that offer help and understanding about SSA (see the list of organizations at the back of the book).
- Teach your religious leaders about the facts of SSA—no one is essentially born this way, they didn't simply choose to have SSA, and change is possible. Perhaps they too were either judgmental about SSA people, or simply endorsed their behavior.
- Teach the facts with love in both your home and place of worship.
- Create a caring community, safe places for all SSA men and women to finally feel loved and accepted.

Photo: Richard Cohen and his youngest son
demonstrating healthy touch.

7. *Healthy touch heals*: Appropriate physical affection is an expression of caring for the other person. An arm around the shoulder, holding a hand, and a healthy hug are acts of love. Most SSA men felt excluded from the world of men while growing up, and many SSA women felt excluded from the

world of women. Listening, learning from them, and caring is the greatest gift you may offer these precious, sensitive souls.

Many of us confuse healthy touch with sex. This confusion is unhealthy and inaccurate. We *can* physically touch without being or becoming sexually intimate. We need to learn to separate a healthy embrace from sex by displaying appropriate physical affection without any thought or desire for sexual intimacy. A strong and genuine hug allows both the giver and receiver to feel a sense of warmth, connection, and love. Practice this first with family members: stand close, look into each other's eyes, and embrace. Breathe, give and receive. Don't rush, keep breathing, giving and receiving. Healthy hugs heal and refresh our soul. Ten hugs a day keeps the doctor away!

Men and women who experience SSA are most often touch-deprived, hungering for physical affection from members of the same gender. Most did not sufficiently bond with their same-gender parent and/or same-gender peers. After going through puberty, those legitimate needs for bonding became eroticized and/or sexualized. Then the world told them, "You are gay," or "You are lesbian." *That is not true.* Their same-sex attractions represent the legitimate need of a child or pre-adolescent for healthy connection with members of the same gender, a sense of belonging, connection and fitting in. In fact, encouraging them to act upon their homosexual inclinations will only obstruct the fulfillment of their basic needs for belonging because those are the needs of a child.

Heterosexual men and women are the solution to this conundrum. Opposite-Sex Attracted (OSA) men, please express healthy male love and physical affection toward SSA men. OSA women please embrace SSA women. Hugging, an arm around the shoulder, walking hand in hand by two men or two women is normal in the Middle East, Asia, and other parts of the world. Unfortunately, we in the Western world have long equated touch with sex. This distortion has made many men oversexed and women undernourished. If you are able to give the gift of a healthy embrace to a SSA man or woman, you may help restore and save someone's life. Simple acts of affection—hugging, arm around the shoulder, or just being buddies with a SSA man, close to a SSA woman—this is something they may have never experienced in their lives.

A word to the wise: Do not expect that because you are now genuinely displaying tender, loving care, they will turn around and become straight! *Once healing begins, change follows.* It took many years for this sensitive soul to develop SSA. Therefore, it will take time to heal their wounds and fill their bucket with healthy love. Be patient, and keep loving.

It bears repeating: *Once healing begins, change follows.* You don't need to worry about changing anyone else but yourself. God will do the changing, not us. Our job is to be there for this wonderful man or woman, showing unconditional love.

The homosexual community is embracing these wounded children, providing a "safe" place for them to share their heartaches and needs. *Straight and late* is how most of us have been. Let's start now, beginning to turn the tide by offering our hearts, hands, and homes to those who experience SSA, whether they choose to change or not.

Offer Love that Will Last

Statistically, homosexual relationships do not last. If they do stay together, most male partners agree to have sex outside their relationship: "The expectation for outside sexual activity was the rule for male couples and exception for heterosexuals" (David McWhirter and Andrew Mattison, *The Male Couple*, Prentice-Hall, New Jersey, 1984, p. 3). Many recent studies confirm this fact. One of Germany's leading sexologists, a self-proclaimed homosexual and university lecturer Dr. Martin Dannecker, published a study. Out of 900 male respondents living in a steady relationship, 83% (747 respondents) said they had had frequent homosexual contacts outside their steady relationships within the last 12 months (Dannecker, M: "Der homosexuelle Mann in Zeichen von Aids," Hamburg 1991, p. 103.). "Open relationship" is the norm for many gay couples. They agree to have sex outside of their partnership.

In *The Sexual Organization of the City,* University of Chicago sociologist Edward Laumann argues that "typical gay city inhabitants spend most of their adult lives in 'transactional' relationships, or short-term commitments of less than six months" (Adrian Brune, "City Gays Skip Long-term Relationships: Study Says," *Washington Blade,* February 27, 2004, p. 12.).

According to the Gay Therapy Center in San Francisco, a study of 517 men surveyed in December 2020, about 42% of gay men in open relationships tell their primary partners about other sexual contacts that they have, while 33% operate under a "don't ask, don't tell" policy (https://www.them.us/story/30-percent-gay-men-open-relationships-new-study).

"The Dutch study of partnered homosexuals, which was published in the journal *AIDS,* found that men with a steady partner had an average of eight sexual partners per year" (Maria Xiridou, et al, "The Contribution of Steady and Casual Partnerships to the Incidence of HIV Infection among Homosexual Men in Amsterdam," *AIDS* 17 (2003): 1031).

When a SSA man begins to internalize the love of many OSA men, his love tank will become more and more filled. This in turn will begin to transform his inner being, and eventually his need for homosexual relationships will naturally wane. Once again, one and one equals two. When a man finally internalizes his sense of masculinity, he will naturally be attracted to that which is different, a woman.

A fellow therapist of mine told me about a former client. This man was an active homosexual and lived with his male partner. He had no intention of coming out of homosexuality, he just wanted to deal with certain issues in his life. During the course of therapy, two men at this work (he was the owner and boss) began to shower him with affection. They were very physical, putting their arms around him at various times, and invited him out for a drink, or just to pal around.

As these relationships continued and he felt more accepted by OSA guys, this self-identified gay man began to feel increasingly ill-at-ease with his partner, and asked him to move into another room in the house as he no longer wanted a physical relationship. Over time, as the intimacy and healthy bonding occurred with his two OSA friends, eventually he asked his partner to leave and they broke up. Yes, his SSA gradually diminished as he too worked on unresolved issues of his past, and eventually opposite-sex attractions ensued!

Standing in the gap, as loving mentors, friends, brothers and sisters is the solution to the homosexual dilemma.

- Heterosexual men are the antidote to help SSA men heal their sense of masculinity.
- Heterosexual women are the antidote to help SSA women heal their sense of femininity.

If you disagree with homosexual behavior, do not harp on this. Judgment never works. I promise you will lose your friend or loved one to the homosexual community. Judgment never works because they are already detached and disconnected, looking for unattained love through someone of the same gender. *Win his heart, and the head will follow.* The world told them, "You're born gay," and that's that. We know this is *not* true, but they don't know this yet. As they seek love through same-sex relationships, your love will stand the test of time, while most homosexual relationships are short lived. Be the last one standing, embrace with all your heart and you will help save a life.

> # This is a battle of love.
> # Whoever loves the most and the longest wins!
> # Never Give Up.

Conclusion

The media, movies and television continue to mislead us, not only about the nature of homosexuality, but also about the nature of conflict resolution. The constant, ongoing, never-ending battles between good and evil through violence creates a lose-lose scenario. It only perpetuates a sick system—fighting begets fighting begets fighting. It will never end. No matter who is wrong or right, no battle will ever generate lasting change because hurting people continue to hurt people.

Martin Luther King, Jr., Mahatma Ghandi, and Nelson Mandela got it right! They knew that only through non-violent resistance, by forgiving those who wronged them, and through embracing one's seeming opposition, lasting change will occur.

Why? Because there is no "evil" per se behind harsh or unkind actions; *there is only lack of love.* Fighting among individuals and couples, within families, between neighbors, religions, races, and nations is really about the same thing: "Do I feel loved, accepted, and cared for, or do I feel rejected?"

> *Ignorance and lack of love are the enemy.*

At the conclusion of the movie, *The Dark Crystal*, a successful resolution was fulfilled when opposing forces joined together to form a whole. Then the darkness in the land was ended and the light shown bright. This is our cue how to reconcile with anyone who experiences SSA.

> *Change ensues when healing occurs.*

Many people believe they must fight *against* homosexual legislation—homosexual marriage rights, homosexual adoption rights, homosexuals in the military, homosexual education in public schools, homosexual clergy, etc. Others fight *for* homosexual persons to have all these rights. I believe that both approaches will ultimately fail. As we have seen in many European countries that fully accept, legalize and endorse homosexual behavior, many of these same-sex attracted men and women are still quite unhappy in their personal lives. Simply fighting against homosexual legislation will not solve this dilemma.

We can either be part of the problem by not taking any action, or we can participate in changing history by reaching out in love, forgiveness, and understanding.

The homosexual issue will not be solved by politics, science, media, or education. The solution is in your hands, within your heart, inside your mind, and by your actions. The sooner we get involved, the sooner the resolution occurs. It is up to you and me to reach out, listen, love, and be the last one standing.

> Here is a Formula to Resolve the Homosexual Dilemma: 1 – 1 – 1
>
> One person, or one family, love one SSA man or woman.
> Then the homosexual issue would become a non-issue.
> Love is the medicine to heal all pain. Love one SSA person.
> Stand with him or her.
> This will transform lives and end political, educational,
> scientific, and religious strife.

Whether I am right or wrong regarding the causes of homosexuality is of no consequence. If I am right, and setting love in order works—men embracing SSA men, and women embracing SSA women—then those who experience same-sex attraction will naturally heal and come out straight. If I am wrong, it is still a win-win scenario, as all persons who experience SSA will finally be heard, healed, and embraced by their family and friends. The simple acts of listening, loving, and being the last one standing in the life of a SSA person will be life-changing.

As Dr. Martin Luther King commissioned, "Darkness cannot drive out darkness; only light can do that. Hate cannot drive out hate; only love can do that." Once again, I mentioned in the introduction to this book, "Truth without love is blind, and love without truth is deadly." Forgive, understand, and love with all *your* heart!

Many use the so-called, "love argument," promoted by homosexual activists and their followers in the media, entertainment industry, political and religious communities. It goes something like this:

> "Love is love. We must love and accept all gays without trying to make them change because they are born this way. We must give them the same rights for marriage and adoption as all heterosexual couples. Let them live as they want. Stop hurting gays! God is love. Love is love."

This is blind love because it denies the very fact that people are not created with SSA. Love fills the sails of the ship, but without the rudder of truth it will go astray. Having same-sex attraction is a symptom of much deeper unresolved issues. Truth without love is blind, because it does not see into the heart of men and women who experience SSA. Love without truth is deadly, because it may lead someone into a life that will ultimately betray them. There are consequences to homosexual behavior, e.g., HIV, AIDS, higher rates of drug and alcohol addiction, high rates of suicide. Many activists will say this is because of socialized prejudice. This is only partly true, because unhealthy behaviors are symptoms of the underlying causes that led someone to experience SSA. In the Netherlands, where homosexual behavior is legal and endorsed by every facet of society, researchers have found a higher incidence of mental illness, and drug and alcohol addiction within the homosexual community than in the heterosexual community. Having all the same "rights" as heterosexuals did not solve their internal conflicts. We need to address this crisis with love and truth in equal measure.

There *is* another side to tolerance, as taught by the gay activists, that is understanding the real facts about SSA and loving in the right ways. "I love you. I know that there is a deeper truth behind your SSA. I am here for you. I love you just as you are. I will stand with you no matter what."

What if it were *you*, or your *child*, or your *parent*, or your *friend*, or your *pastor, priest, rabbi, imam* or *neighbor?* Homosexual activists did what most people of good conscience and faith failed to do. They taught us to treat SSA men and women with dignity and respect. Most people of faith failed to do that until homosexual activists brought the issue out of the "closet." Now, in the name of tolerance, diversity, and equality, the truth has been suppressed. This is to the detriment of everyone who experiences SSA and their loved ones.

Let us work together to end the hate and to end the hurtful comments about anyone who experiences SSA. It's time to step up to the plate and listen, love, and last. *Whoever loves the most and the longest will win.* Let us preserve the family—one man and one woman—by learning to love those who experience SSA the right way!

If you feel inspired, get involved with SSA healing ministries and organizations (see the list at the back of the book). Make a difference. They need to hear from people like you, so please support organizations that are doing this type of work.

...the greatest of these is love...

A chain is only as strong as its weakest link. If every church, synagogue, temple and mosque would launch a **Love One SSA Person Campaign**, all this nonsense would be over.

Imagine the impact of one family mentoring one SSA person for one year, whether s/he chooses to change or not. Whatever the outcome, love is the medicine that will heal that person's pain. By demonstrating real love, by helping to heal their heart and soul, we know that remarkable and lasting change will ensue.

Remember the concluding remarks of *After the Ball*: "keep your rage, we cannot tolerate injustice." Let us help dissipate their rage. We have to show all persons who experience SSA the right kinds of love to soften and win their hearts. It starts by one person loving another, by one family mentoring a SSA man or woman. Let us be catalysts for change in the world.

Recommended Reading

Male Homosexuality

1. *Being Gay: Nature, Nurture, or Both?* Richard Cohen, M.A., PATH Press, Bowie, MD, 2020.
2. *Reparative Therapy of Male Homosexuality,* Joseph Nicolosi, Ph.D., Jason Aaronson, Inc., 1991
3. *Shame and Attachment Loss: The Practical Work of Reparative Therapy,* Joseph Nicolosi, Ph.D., 2016.
4. *Growth into Manhood,* Alan Medinger, WaterBrook Press (Shaw), Colorado Springs, CO, 2000.
5. *Practical Exercises for Men in Recovery of Same-Sex Attraction,* James Phelan, Psy.D, Morris Publishing, Kearney, NE, 2006.

Female Homosexuality

6. *The Heart of Female Same-Sex Attraction: A Comprehensive Counseling Resource,* Janelle Hallman, InterVarsity Press, Downers Grove, IL, 2008.
7. *Restoring Sexual Identity: Hope for Women Who Struggle with Same-Sex Attraction,* Anne Paulk, Harvest House, Eugene, OR, 2003.
8. *Female Homosexuality: Choice without Volition,* Elaine V. Siegel, Ph.D., Analytic Press, Hillsdale, NJ, 1988.

9. *Practical Exercises for Women in Recovery of Same-Sex Attraction*, James Phelan, Debora Barr, Phelan Consultants, 2011.

10. *All Things New: A Former Lesbian's Lifelong Search for Love*, Debora Barr, True Potential Publisher, 2013.

Family / Friends

11. *Gay Children, Straight Parents: A Plan for Family Healing*, Richard Cohen, M.A., PATH Press, Bowie, MD, 2016.

12. *A Parent's Guide to Preventing Homosexuality*, Joseph Nicolosi, Ph.D., Liberal Mind Pub., 2017

13. *Out from Under: The Impact of Homosexual Parenting*, Dawn Stefanowicz, Annotation Press, Enumclaw, WA, 2007.

General Books on Homosexuality

14. *My Genes Made Me Do It: A Scientific Look at Sexual Orientation*, Neil and Briar Whitehead, Huntington House Publishers, Lafayette, LA, 1999. Updated 2020.

15. *You Don't Have to Be Gay: Hope and Freedom for Males Struggling with Homosexuality*, Jeff Conrad, Pacific Publishing House, Newport Beach, CA, 2001.

16. *Desires in Conflict: Answering the Struggle for Sexual Identity*, Joe Dallas, Harvest House, Eugene, OR, 1991.

Political Influence of Homosexuality in the American Psychiatric Association

17. *Homosexuality and American Psychiatry*, Ronald Bayer, Princeton University Press, Princeton, NJ, 1981.

18. *Homosexuality and the Politics of Truth*, Jeffrey Satinover, M.D., Baker Books, 1996.

Organizations*

Therapeutic Organizations:

- The Alliance for Therapeutic Choice and Scientific Integrity
  https://www.therapeuticchoice.com
- Positive Approaches To Healthy Sexuality (PATH)
  www.pathinfo.org
- American College of Pediatricians
  www.FactsAboutYouth.com

Faith Ministries for SSA:

- Joel 225 (Online support groups for those with unwanted
  SSA in many languages)
  www.joel225.org
- Brothers Road (On-line support groups for men / JIM
  weekend experience)
  https://www.brothersroad.org
- PFOX: Parents and Friends of Ex-Gays and Gays (Christian)
  www.pfox.org
- Restored Hope Network (Christian support for those with
  unwanted SSA & loved ones)
  www.restoredhopenetwork.com
- Courage / Encourage (Catholic)
  www.couragerc.net

- North Star (Mormon)
  www.northstarlds.org
- Strong Support (Muslim)
  https://www.strongsupport.co.uk
- Homosexuals Anonymous (Christian)
  http://www.ha-fs.org
- One by One (Presbyterian)
  www.oneby1.org
- Exgay Calling (Scientific Understanding of SSA)
  https://exgaycalling.com
- Wife's support groups:
  http://www.brothersroad.org/whj/helpforwives/

Children of Gay Parents Organization:

- Support for children of LGBTQ+ parents
  http://dawnstefanowicz.com

Testimonies of Change

- www.voicesofchange.net

*Contact info of these organizations change frequently. Check their websites for updates.

About the Author

Richard Cohen, M.A., is a psycho-therapist, educator, and author who travels throughout the United States, Europe, Latin America, and the Middle East teaching about marital relations, parenting skills, healing from sexual abuse, and understanding gender identity and sexual orientation issues. Over the past 35 years, he has helped hundreds in therapy and thousands through healing seminars, as well as trained over 6,000 physicians, psychologists, counselors, and ministry leaders how to assist those dealing with gender identity and sexual orientation concerns.

Cohen is the author of 1) *Being Gay: Nature, Nurture or Both?*, 2) *Gay Children Straight Parents: A Plan for Family Healing*, 3) *Understanding Our LGBTQ+ Loved Ones*, 4) *Healing Humanity: Time, Touch, and Talk.*, 5) *Counselor Training Program Film Series: Assisting Those with Same-Sex Attraction and Their Loved Ones*, and 6) *Rich's Home*. His books are published in thirteen languages.

He founded the International Healing Foundation (IHF) in 1990, and is currently the president and co-founder of Positive Approaches To Healthy Sexuality (PATH). Based in the Washington, D.C. metropolitan area, PATH offers counselor training programs, family healing sessions, consultations, resource materials, and speaking engagements.

Cohen holds a Bachelor's degree from Boston University and a Master's of Arts degree in counseling psychology from Antioch University. For three years, he worked as an HIV/AIDS educator for the Seattle King County, Washington chapter of the American Red Cross where he authored a statewide curriculum for foster parents and health care providers dealing with HIV infected children.

Cohen has been interviewed by newspaper, radio and television media including appearances on *20/20, Jimmy Kimmel Live, Rachel Maddow, Larry King Live, CNN,* and other news outlets throughout the world. He lives in the Washington, D.C., metropolitan area with his wife of forty-two years, while his three adult children are making their mark on the world.

Positive Approaches To Healthy Sexuality (PATH)
P.O. Box 2315, Bowie, MD 20715 / Tel. (301) 805-5155
Email: pathinfo@pathinfo.org
www.pathinfo.org
www.TimeTouchandTalk.com

Printed in Great Britain
by Amazon

24109861R00119